VOLUME 21

ACTS

James E. Sargent

ABINGDON PRESS
Nashville

Acts

This book is printed on recycled, acid-free paper.

Library of Congress Cataloging-in-Publication Data

Cokesbury basic Bible commentary.
  Basic Bible commentary / by Linda B. Hinton . . . [et.al.].
    p. cm.
  Originally published: Cokesbury basic Bible commentary. Nashville: Graded Press, © 1988.
  ISBN 0-687-02620-2 (pbk. : v. 1 : alk. paper)
  1. Bible—Commentaries. I. Hinton, Linda B. II. Title.
  [BS491.2.C65 1994]
  220.7—dc20   94-10965
                                                                                CIP

ISBN 0-687-02640-7 (v. 21, Acts)
ISBN 0-687-02620-2 (v. 1, Genesis)
ISBN 0-687-02621-0 (v. 2, Exodus–Leviticus)
ISBN 0-687-02622-9 (v. 3, Numbers–Deuteronomy)
ISBN 0-687-02623-7 (v. 4, Joshua–Ruth)
ISBN 0-687-02624-5 (v. 5, 1–2 Samuel)
ISBN 0-687-02625-3 (v. 6, 1–2 Kings)
ISBN 0-687-02626-1 (v. 7, 1–2 Chronicles)
ISBN 0-687-02627-X (v. 8, Ezra–Esther)
ISBN 0-687-02628-8 (v. 9, Job)
ISBN 0-687-02629-6 (v. 10, Psalms)
ISBN 0-687-02630-X (v. 11, Proverbs–Song of Solomon)
ISBN 0-687-02631-8 (v. 12, Isaiah)
ISBN 0-687-02632-6 (v. 13, Jeremiah–Lamentations)
ISBN 0-687-02633-4 (v. 14, Ezekiel–Daniel)
ISBN 0-687-02634-2 (v. 15, Hosea–Jonah)
ISBN 0-687-02635-0 (v. 16, Micah–Malachi)
ISBN 0-687-02636-9 (v. 17, Matthew)
ISBN 0-687-02637-7 (v. 18, Mark)
ISBN 0-687-02638-5 (v. 19, Luke)
ISBN 0-687-02639-3 (v. 20, John)
ISBN 0-687-02642-3 (v. 22, Romans)
ISBN 0-687-02643-1 (v. 23, 1–2 Corinthians)
ISBN 0-687-02644-X (v. 24, Galatians–Ephesians)
ISBN 0-687-02645-8 (v. 25, Philippians–2 Thessalonians)
ISBN 0-687-02646-6 (v. 26, 1 Timothy–Philemon)
ISBN 0-687-02647-4 (v. 27, Hebrews)
ISBN 0-687-02648-2 (v. 28, James–Jude)
ISBN 0-687-02649-0 (v. 29, Revelation)
ISBN 0-687-02650-4 (complete set of 29 vols.)

98 99 00 01 02 03—10 9 8 7 6 5 4 3

Contents

Outline of Acts

10. The brethren are silenced (11:18)
11. A mission to the Greeks (11:19-26)
12. Christian famine relief (11:27-30)
H. Herodian Persecution (12:1-25)
1. Herod Agrippa's persecution begins (12:1-4)
2. A miraculous escape for Peter (12:5-19)
3. The death of Herod Agrippa (12:20-23)
4. Paul's first missionary journey (12:24-25)

II. Part Two (13:1–28:31)
A. The First Missionary Journey (13:1–14:28)
1. Barnabas and Saul called to mission (13:1-5)
2. Encounter with a magician (13:6-15)
3. Paul's sermon (13:16-41)
4. Trouble brewing (13:42-47)
5. The mission continues (13:48-52)
6. A plot develops (14:1-5)
7. The disciples flee (14:6-7)
8. A cripple is healed (14:8-14)
9. Paul's protest (14:15-18)
10. Return to Antioch (14:19-28)
B. The Jerusalem Conference (15:1-35)
1. The controversy is stated (15:1-5)
2. Elders gather; Peter's speech (15:6-11)
3. Description of the Gentile mission (15:12-21)
4. Representatives sent to Antioch (15:22-29)
5. Victory for the Gentile mission (15:30-35)
C. The Second Missionary Journey Begins (15:36-41)
D. The Second Missionary Journey (16:1–18:22)
1. Derbe and Lystra (16:1-5)
2. Phrygia, Galatia, and Troas (16:6-10)
3. In Philippi (16:11-15)
4. Conflict and arrest (16:16-24)
5. Imprisonment and vindication (16:25-40)
6. To Thessalonica (17:1-9)
7. A narrow escape (17:10-15)
8. Paul in Athens (17:16-21)

Introduction to Acts

Acts is a daring sequel to the gospel witness of the life and work of Jesus. Acts is the only book that continues the narrative of the work of Jesus through the church and the apostles. Originally the book was part of a larger corpus of material (see Acts 1:1). When the New Testament canon was formed the first volume, the Gospel of Luke, was placed with the three other Gospels. Acts was placed following the Fourth Gospel. Its placement indicates its function as it links the life of Jesus with the letters of Paul.

The Author or Acts

The author of the book of Acts has traditionally been identified as Luke, the beloved physician (see 2 Timothy 4:11, Colossians 4:14, Philemon 24 where Luke is mentioned). The book is addressed to *Theophilus*, which in Greek means *lover of God*. Therefore, the work could easily have been intended for a single reader's eye.

On the other hand, the tone of the work is clearly apologetic. The book could easily have been a work intended to place the Christian faith and church in a positive light before the Roman authorities. In that case, Theophilus could have been a patron of the early Christian movement. All attempts at identification of the book's original audience are matters of conjecture, since we simply cannot ascertain for certain the individual or individuals to whom the work is addressed. One thing is certain, however. The work is read by Christians as a

7

stirring account of the initial moments in the life of the Christian movement.

The Date of Acts

Any attempt to date the writing is equally frustrating. No evidence within the book itself gives specific years. The tone of defense and apologetic imply a time when the church was under great stress, possibly persecution. A good number of episodes in the book of Acts give strong encouragement to those under stress. But a specific date simply cannot be determined. Scholars do conclude that the work was written sometime late in the first century.

The Purpose of Acts

Much more important than who the author was, the identity of the individual called Theophilus, or the time of the writing, is the purpose of the work. Obviously, the overriding purpose is that of edification of Christian believers. *It seemed good also to me* (NIV) or *I too decided* (NRSV) (Luke 1:3) implies that corrective with respect to doctrine or tradition was necessary to a degree. Since much of the second half of the work centers on the trial and defense of Paul, the purpose could well have been to defend Paul as representative of all Christianity. One scholar suggests that the book is an attempt to recover the reputation of Paul.

Certainly a reading of Acts gives a different perspective from what Paul's own letters reveal. In Acts, the great apostle strides across the Mediterranean—in sharp contrast to the beleaguered preacher and struggling apostle portrayed in the epistles.

Throughout the work divine guidance is emphasized. The reason is quite clear. The early church impetus towards expansion could not be the result merely of individuals who wanted to direct the fortunes of the believing community. The expansion had to be the result of God's own intention and direction. This in turn gives justification for the mission to the Gentiles. Perhaps no other single purpose is as clear or important in Acts as the legitimacy of the Gentile mission.

The Theology of Acts

Theological concerns to which the writer addresses himself include the expected return of Jesus. Christians felt that Jesus' return was imminent. At any moment all of history could come to its grand conclusion with the return of Jesus. The delay of the return posed a special problem for the early church. Indeed, Acts begins with a scene intended to dispel sky-gazing expectation.

Unlike other writings in the New Testament, the book of Acts contains no systematic presentation of major topics in Christian thinking. At no time is any complete treatise presented regarding God, Jesus, the church, or even the Holy Spirit. Throughout the work passages can be found in which these issues are mentioned. But any organized formulation of theological issues is largely accidental.

The work of the Holy Spirit does occupy a major place in Acts. However, the work of the Spirit is varied and never fits into categories or systems. Some readers may want to find in these pages the Holy Spirit working with pure spontaneity. Indeed, there are moments of spontaneity and ecstasy. However, a good deal of the Holy Spirit's work is challenging, confrontive, directive, and stern. The early church struggled long and hard not only within itself but with its Lord as well with regard to the mission to those outside the law. At every important point in the church's history the Holy Spirit prevails and the church reaches out to its ultimate destination: a universal gospel.

How to Read Acts

Modern readers will face certain difficulties when reading Acts. The reason for this is quite simple. We want to use familiar categories of thought and expression. But Acts is an ancient book and therefore uses ancient customs and conventions. Miracles, for instance, are sprinkled throughout the work—people are healed, both through a touch and by the mere passing of Peter's shadow. A young boy is brought back to life by the apostle Paul. A poisonous snake can do no harm to Paul on Malta. Prisoners are released from prison by earthquake and angels—for the ancient Israelites these incidents are not unusual at all.

Such stories are central in Christian thinking. But for modern readers they are difficult. We must remember to consider the abiding human experience that these peculiar images or categories address. We will be a good deal closer to an appropriate use of the Bible if we can allow the ancient methods to express something that is true in human nature and in God's work with the creation. We must resist the temptation to rationalize everything away for scientific or logical reasons.

Similarly, ancient historical methods include speeches or sermons that were not mere verbatim reports. Composite speeches were common in the ancient world. Again, the writer is not concerned solely with strict reporting of events and statements. Luke's concern is the meaning of events and beliefs contained in the sermons. Another ancient convention is that of using a specific incident as representative of a larger phenomenon. For instance, there were many more encounters between Christians and Samaritans than the single incident reported by Luke. However, the intention is accomplished. The reader will understand that single events stand for widespread occurrences.

At times the writer does not quote the Hebrew Scriptures exactly. For some readers such incidents are errors and thereby call into question the authority of the Bible. Such a perspective, however, is shortsighted.

The writer did not have at his disposal fine libraries with multiple volumes that were cross-indexed. He had only the material at hand, recollections saved through storytelling, his own reminiscences, and the memorized Scriptures. Again, ancient readers would not have balked at slight misquotations of Scripture.

The same insight should be kept in mind with respect to some details that appear either contradictory or incredible. Luke's purpose was not to present a seamless weave of exact history. We can almost see his excitement grow as he tells the dramatic story of how the church grew from a few frightened souls to the victorious faith that reached even Rome itself!

Finally, we must remember that Luke's purpose was to tell the story of the movement of Christianity beyond the bounds of race, tradition, and culture. Therefore, if we attempt to make this work serve as an anvil on which to work out systematic theological formulations, we overstep Luke's intention.

The Meaning of Acts

The development of the book of Acts underscores its purpose. Beginning in Jerusalem with a handful of believers, the gospel moves steadily outward. It travels first from Jerusalem to the Gentile world. Then it moves from Aramaic-speaking converts to Gentile converts. Through the work of Peter and Paul the gospel makes its way to the masses of people populating the entire known world.

When we ask the question, What is the book of Acts about? The answer might well be, *Acts is about the inevitable work of God to spread the gospel of Christ to every corner of the world.*

An image may help. Nearly everyone has stood at the edge of a pond, thrown a stone into the middle of the water, and watched the ripples reach the shore line.

In a way the book of Acts shows the initial splash of the ministry of Jesus. Inevitably, and without regard for resistance, the Holy Spirit propels the gospel into both the far reaches of human imagination and the geographical expanse of the Roman Empire.

PART ONE

Acts 1-2

Introduction to These Chapters

The first two chapters of Acts introduce the reader to both a remarkable document and a series of events. The book itself is a continuation of the work of Jesus. No other such book survives. We have no other record. The history to which it gives witness is that of the apostolic age. Three major events form the content of these chapters: the risen Christ (the Resurrection); Christ's ascension; and finally the unprecedented phenomenon of Pentecost.

Throughout the book of Acts the presence and work of the Holy Spirit are primary concerns. However, Luke also attempts to present a complete or systematic theology of the Spirit. The narrative of how the Christian message spread quickens the imagination as the expansion of Christianity has to work through internal as well as external resistance.

Here is an outline of chapters 1 and 2:
I. Introduction of the Risen Christ (1:1-5)
II. The Ascension (1:6-11)
III. The Apostles in Jerusalem (1:12-26)
IV. Pentecost (2:1-42)
    A. Introduction (2:1–4)
    B. Mighty Work Understood by All (2:5-13)
    C. Peter's Interpretation and Sermon (2:14-36)
    D. Response to the Preached Word (2:37-42)
V. A Description of the Early Church (2:43-47)

Introduction of the Risen Christ

Theophilus means *lover of God or God-fearer*. In either case the Roman authority or the patron is clearly sympathetic to the Christian movement.

Since the author refers to an earlier book, the Gospel of Luke, we can assume that the process of organizing authoritative materials—that process is called *canonization*—had already begun even at this very early stage in the church's history. The book of Acts continues the drama of Jesus' work.

Throughout Acts the writer emphasizes that Jesus himself authorizes and directs the Christian movement. Luke immediately establishes Jesus' authority by characterizing the disciples as chosen by Jesus. However, the disciples as well as others in the church will struggle with the direction in which Jesus leads.

The task to which Jesus assigns the apostles is of such magnitude as to require sufficient preparation and strength. Thus, the apostles are instructed to wait in the city for the promised Holy Spirit.

The baptism of the Holy Spirit differs from the baptism of John. John's baptism was characterized by repentance and water. John's baptism could be refused, and on occasion John did refuse to baptize. The baptism of the Spirit is not so much a physical event as it is a moment when a greater power is realized in and through those who are already Christian.

The Ascension (1:6-11)

The apostles had already talked with Jesus about the Kingdom of God during the intervening forty days. Now their question sounds with the effect of a thunderclap. When will the Kingdom come and Israel be restored? The question betrays a long-held nationalistic hope with an implied narrowness of vision. It also implies a sharp anxiety about when this end-time event will occur. The word that is used for the end time is *eschatology*. Early

Christians fervently anticipated the end of the age. Would it come with the arrival of the Spirit? Would the Kingdom be limited to the nation of Israel? This theme of national aspiration will be repeated over and over again throughout Acts as resistance to the wider, more universal missionary efforts.

Jesus' response confronts the apostles: They are not to know the time. Furthermore, the mission for the apostles will transcend national boundaries. Indeed, the movement will reach the ends of the earth. For this enterprise the apostles will be given the Holy Spirit. These are Jesus' last words on earth.

The word *ascension* is never used in the Scripture. Instead, the church's tradition has assigned this term to describe the event. The description of the event itself is quite reserved in contrast to Elijah's ascension on the whirlwind with the flaming chariot. Jesus merely disappears into the clouds. Luke seems unconcerned about providing an explanation. Evidently the apostles' attitude is the focus of these verses. They, like all early Christians, desired and expected Jesus' imminent return. The ascension is important because it further demonstrates the fact of the Resurrection, and now the apostles can receive the Holy Spirit.

Still stunned by Jesus' words and the ascension, the apostles stand staring at the clouds. Two angles appear. They challenge the apostles. In doing so they are also challenging the entire early church's attitude towards the return (Parousia) of Jesus. Preoccupation with the return is inappropriate. The church at Thessalonica develops just such a preoccupation and is subsequently corrected by Paul (see 2 Thessalonians 3:6-15). The apostles are instructed to return to Jerusalem.

The Apostles in Jerusalem (1:12-26)

The eleven gather in the Upper Room. With the exception of Peter and John, other names do not appear in the balance of the book, though James' death is reported in Acts 12:2. The family of Jesus is mentioned but not by specific names. Mary is mentioned only one time in Acts. Thus two groups are listed: apostles, who became a nucleus of the congregation of Jerusalem; and others, not apostles.

Initially the entire Christian congregation is shown in remarkable unity. They number 120, a full complement. Most of them are Galileans gathered in Jerusalem.

Christian traditions vary in describing the fate of Judas. In Matthew, Judas hangs himself. The important fact, however, is not how Judas died. Rather, what is most important is the ongoing work of Jesus.

Peter occupies central importance throughout the first half of Acts, beginning with this interpretation.

Judas' vacancy must be filled by someone who meets three requirements: (1) he must be a man who followed Jesus from his baptism by John to the ascension; (2) he must be an eyewitness to the Resurrection; and (3) he must have the authorization of Jesus and must have been appointed by Jesus (1:24). For Luke, the Resurrection is absolutely essential to the Christian faith.

The human factor is excluded in selection of Matthias; God does the choosing.

Pentecost (2:1-42)

Pentecost is fifty days following the Passover. Formerly an agricultural festival, Pentecost has evolved additionally into a celebration of the giving of the Law, or Torah.

Introduction (2:1-4)

Spectacular phenomena accompany the presence of the Spirit: first sound, then tongues of fire, then ecstatic utterances. Modern Christians are frequently inclined to make both more or less of the event than it really was. They make more of it by overemphasizing the audio and visual signs. These signs are not mentioned anywhere else in the New Testament. They make less of the event by overlooking the fact that the signs are temporary. The presence and the power are the abiding realities.

Mighty Work Understood by All (2:5-13)

The ecstatic utterance is not unintelligible speech. Foreign Jews hear in their own particular languages. A listing of the nations from which Jews had gathered gives evidence of the remarkable fact that Galilean Jews spoke various languages (2:14-36). Peter preaches in response to mocking demands made by opponents.

Peter's Interpretation and Sermon (2:14-36)

Since Peter is addressing primarily Jews, he can use Hebrew Scripture as a reference. He alludes to Joel 2:28-32. Joel, however, makes no mention of foreign languages.

Central in Christian preaching is the crucifixion of Jesus. The notion of a crucified messiah offended all who desired a military commander who would triumphantly right all the wrongs of the world. But the crucifixion readily concedes to the victory of the Resurrection. Luke's presentation of the Passion is not one of Jesus caught in an accidental series of horrible events. Jesus realized what the cost of redemption would be. The climax of the sermon is, therefore, resurrection. The entire drama fulfills Scripture.

The term used for early Christian preaching is *kerygma*. Peter's sermon contains many of the essential elements of the kerygma:

1. prophecies in Scripture fulfilled (2:17-21)
2. Jesus born of the seed of David (2:25)
3. Jesus died to deliver us, according to Scripture
4. Jesus was buried
5. Jesus rose

6. Jesus is exalted at the right hand of God (2:33)

7. Jesus will come again.

Response to the Preached Word (2:37-42)

An appropriate response to preaching is repentance. Baptism is not necessarily required for the promise of the Holy Spirit. That is, an outward sign or action is not required.

Four disciplines characterize the early Christians: (1) instruction by the apostles; (2) contribution of offering; (3) communal meals; (4) prayers.

The Christian movement is one of great vigor and vitality among Jews who continue to be a part of their Temple. Thus far Christians have evoked little resistance.

A Description of the Early Church (2:43-47)

Luke summarizes through vivid and concise images and scenes what would otherwise require a great deal more time and space. Other similar summaries will occur later on in the book of Acts (4:32-35; 5:12-15). The new Christian community centers on a shared common life that is celebrated regularly. Evidently the power of this way of living attracts thousands of converts within a very short time.

§ § § § § § §

The Message of Acts 1–2

These two chapters recount remarkable events and truths. The power and truth is not restricted to a single historical era. We must ask what the significance of these events is for our generation as well as for the early church. What, then, do these chapters tell us about God and God's work with us?

§   Election is by God.
§   The task of Christianity is not to passively await Christ's return. Rather, Christians must establish new relationships to the world in which they live.
§   The real boundaries are never geographical; they are religious, national, and racial.
§   The Holy Spirit sometimes breaks up comfortable and familiar patterns.
§   God's summons is both filled with promise and laden with responsibility.
§   God's power exceeds even the power of death.
§   Christ will return.
§   The Holy Spirit is available to all.
§   The Christian community is characterized by its care, discipline, and prayer.

§ § § § § § §

Acts 3–4

Introduction to These Chapters

Chapters 3 and 4 continue with the stories of miraculous works by the apostles. Earlier we saw the vigorous movement attracting large numbers of people. Doubtless there were more events than Luke could possibly include in the text of this single volume. Therefore, he has to use stories that not only illustrate the unprecedented impact of Christ but also represent many other similar events. We will see this technique illustrated in later chapters.

Here is an outline of these chapters:

Peter Heals a Lame Man (3:1-10)

Luke points out that the apostles are still pious men of deep tradition. They are still attending synagogue services. Miraculous healing confirms the presence of the Holy Spirit. The fact that the man had been crippled all of his life underscores the power of the Holy Spirit.

The *Beautiful Gate* (NRSV) or *gate called Beautiful* (NIV) is known traditionally as the Shusha Gate that led to the east side of the Temple.

The significance of the miraculous healing goes beyond a remedy for one physical impairment. Since the Holy Spirit is a power, it translates into the moral realm as well. Clearly the story implies that what has been accomplished in the physical realm with birth can be accomplished within people who are in some sense morally disabled. Interpreters of miracles must keep in mind that miracles serve many functions. In Acts salvation is not through miracles, but by grace. Miracles are invitations to both repentance and faith. As in the Gospels, they point beyond themselves to larger realities.

Note that the healing is accomplished without any spectacular action or wild incantations. The mere utterance of Jesus' name is sufficient for divine power to be transmitted. Touch also establishes a channel for power (see Acts 14:8-10, where ankles are healed).

Luke's characterization that all are amazed underscores two facts. First, the miracle is a reality. The man had indeed been changed from a habitual lifestyle of defeat and disability. Second, thus far all who witness the work of the Christian movement are awestruck and favorable to the movement.

Solomon's Portico (NRSV) or *Colonade* (NIV) is on the east side of the Temple as is the Beautiful Gate.

Peter Preaches (3:11-26)

Peter further interprets the Christian message. Initially great care is taken to make sure people understand that the power is not the apostles'. The power is God's and God's alone. The apostles are instruments; God is to be glorified. Righteous religious behavior is not how the power has been evoked, either.

Servant (verse 13) is a biblical term with a rich tradition. Here it is used by Jesus to describe great men of God. Christians adopted the term for Jesus (see Acts 3:26; 4:27, 30).

In this sermon the Jews are held responsible for the death of Jesus. Here Pilate is characterized as wanting to release Jesus. Since the Romans are not blamed for the death of Jesus, many scholars suggest the book of Acts attempts to prove that Christianity is not a threat to Rome. By the same token, all modern readers must avoid anti-Jewish sentiments based on this Scripture passage.

The emphasis is not on the death of Jesus, rather it is on his resurrection. Resurrection is a central element in the kerygma.

Faith must be present if the name of Jesus is to have any real power of authority.

Peter's use of the word *brothers* (NIV) or *friends* (NRSV) implies that there is no need for religious barriers.

The Hebrew word for repentance is *Shuv,* to turn. Repentance is possible for Jews and Gentiles alike. Repentance will hasten the delayed return of Christ, and the promise of all the prophets will finally be realized. Peter contends that any who do not heed Jesus, and presumably the Christian witness to him, will summarily be excluded from the people of God. In this sense the Christian claim is that Christians are the true Israel. The sermon concludes with the call for repentance.

A comment about the speeches and sermons in Acts is appropriate at this time. Many readers will want to know if these are actual, verbatim speeches. In all likelihood they are composite pieces intending to represent typical preaching of the era. Not all sermons followed precisely the same outline. For Luke the sermons are not merely descriptions of preaching, they *are* preaching in their own right.

Peter and John Before the High Council (4:1-4)

Sadducees were nobility and upperclass Jews. They were not technically a class, though they did control the

Jerusalem Temple. Sadducees did not believe in resurrection. Interestingly, the Pharisees did hold to the belief in resurrection. Strictly speaking, therefore, Christianity initially aroused resistance from one group within Judaism. The Pharisees are not yet pictured as opponents.

The number 5,000 is reminiscent of the number Jesus fed by miraculous increase in the Gospels. Here, 5,000 symbolizes the large number of converts to the new and energetic movement.

The Next Day (4:5-7)

The High Council cannot meet until the next day, so the apostles must be held overnight. Composition of the High Council includes Ananias the high priest, Caiaphas, John, and Alexander. Against this high authority the apostles' courage shows clearly.

Again, Peter is the speaker while John remains silent. Here the presence of the Holy Spirit is symbolized by the apostles' power and courage. No other phenomena accompany the presence.

Peter's Speech (4:8-12)

The examination by the Sadducees is characterized as a trial. Peter demands to know why a trial is necessary. Because a man has been healed?

The Apostles' Release (4:13-22)

The name of Jesus is the power by which the malady is cured. The term *salvation* describes healing which can be both physical and spiritual healing.

Sadducees of such high authority are not accustomed to common people exhibiting remarkable courage. Presumably other common folk would be reduced to quivering and fearful subjects. But these men have a distinct strength from the presence of the Spirit.

Though the Sadducees disagree with the apostles'

teaching and feel very threatened by the success of the Christian movement, they must recognize that the lame man has in fact been healed.

The council deliberations reveal men who refuse to be convinced by the miracle. *This name* is the name of Jesus (see also 5:28). Luke uses this miracle story to illustrate the power of Jesus' name. The name links the divine power with people on earth. In Jesus' name sick persons are healed (3:6, 16; 4:7,10); signs and wonders are performed (4:30); people are baptized (2:38; 8:16; 10:48; 19:5). Through his name disciples preach and teach (4:17; 5:28, 40; 8:12; 9:15, 27, 29). Since the name is very powerful, some want to use the name as magic (9:13-20).

The apostles' well-known rejoinder questions the Sadducees' authority. The Sadducees did not have official authority. Indeed, had resurrection been the only issue, the Pharisees too would be censured. The question of authority looms large; and as for the apostles, they will obey only God. Doubtless the Christian community took great courage from this simple affirmation, even in the face of increasing persecution.

The eyewitness authority is placed in contrast to mere official gathering authority. The fact that the man had been lame for his entire life underscores the apostles' witness.

Congregational Thanksgiving (4:23-31)

The scent shifts from the large numbers mentioned in 2:41 and 4:4 to a group that could fit into a single room. The image is that of a small band of courageous and committed men and women.

The congregational prayer alludes to the prophet Isaiah (Isaiah 37:16-20). God as Creator also implies the lordship of God in history. God holds the future of the Christian movement in God's own hands.

Psalm 2:1-2 is used to interpret the current circumstances.

The phrase *kings of the earth* is interpreted to suggest Herod Antipas; the word *rulers* suggests Pilate.

None of what has happened occurred by accident. All is within the purview of God's intention. The current stress requires a boldly preached word of God. The spoken or preached word may be accompanied by healings, signs, and wonders, all of which are done by God. Again, the power of Jesus' name is stated.

At the conclusion of the prayer the building trembles. This could signify that the prayer has been heard. The trembling could also be a parallel to the events of the Pentecost. In either event, the congregation is filled with the Holy Spirit.

Exemplary Christian Behavior (4:32-37)

Recall that Luke uses individual events to illustrate representative events in the life of the church. However, in these verses, the model behavior of Barnabas calls attention to a specific man and to an ideal community attitude towards goods and possessions. Obviously people still had private property. What is remarkable is that some individuals are able give up their claims or right to property. The entire episode may have been preserved because the behavior is unique. Relief work began almost immediately within the Christian movement. We will see how the work malfunctions later on. In fact, the ideal may have differed from reality.

Deuteronomy 15:4 promises "there should be no poor among you."

A *Levite* refers to the tradition of the priestly family.

§ § § § § § §

The Message of Acts 3–4

Interpreters of miracles must keep in mind that miracles serve many functions. In Acts salvation is not through miracles, but by grace. Miracles are invitations to both repentance and faith. As in the Gospels, they point beyond themselves to larger realities.

What can we learn from these chapters?

§ Christians call attention to the remarkable power of God.

§ Christian power is not wealth. It is healing power in the name of Jesus Christ.

§ Salvation comes through the name of Jesus.

§ Prayer asks for sufficient strength for the demand of the hour.

§ Prayer is in response to both courage and strength.

§ Prayer makes no mention of relieving the Christian community from stress or threat of persecutions.

§ Christians show deep care for each other through sharing of goods.

§ § § § § § §

Acts 5–6

Introduction to These Chapters

The euphoric pictures of the church presented in Acts
2:42 where fellowship and prayer characterize the
congregation, and in 4:32-37 (which we read in the
previous chapter) are now shattered by a dreadful
narrative of lies, deceptions, and death. Also, resistance
to the Christian movement increases. Luke skillfully
presents the Christian beginnings through the use of
concise stories and images. In this part of Acts we will
see escalating resistance to the movement, though it does
not yet assume violent proportions.

Here is an outline of chapters 5 and 6:
  I. Ananias and Sapphira Deceive and Lie (5:1-11)
 II. Preaching and Healing Continue (5:12-16)
III. Miracles and Resistance (5:17-26)
 IV. An Appearance Before the Council (5:27-32)
  V. Gamaliel's Wise Counsel (5:33-42)
 VI. Cracks in the Foundation (6:1-4)
VII. Selection of Stephen (6:5-15)

Ananias and Sapphira Deceive and Lie (5:1-11)

The narrative of deception and outright lying by two
members of the Christian movement is a terribly
troubling one. It recalls an equally troubling story in the
Old Testament, that of Achan (see Joshua 7:1-26). Why
would previously faithful members of the congregation

act in such destructive ways? Why does Luke include the story?

Peter speaks for the entire community. Not only does he ask the obvious question as to motive, he poses an issue of far deeper significance. To lie to the apostles or the congregation is to lie to the Holy Spirit. The stakes are raised immensely.

The stunned Ananias falls dead. Some readers may be offended by the abruptness of his death with no chance for repentance. But Luke's purpose is to show the power of God. God executes judgment. All who hear of this dreadful event are awestruck.

As if one death weren't unfortunate enough, Sapphira appears some three hours later. Peter's charge again places the offense against the Holy Spirit. Judgment is again carried out immediately.

Verse 11 gives us a clue as to the meaning of the story. The events are shocking enough to evoke shudders of fear. Perhaps the story was used to teach new converts about the expectations of members and the power of the Holy Spirit. Clearly those with the Holy Spirit in and with them are able to look into the heart of a sinner or deceiver. But these possibilities are secondary to the primary emphasis, which is on God and God's power.

The story also serves as a mirror. It reflects discord and stress within the church that parallels the increasing stress coming to bear on the movement from without.

A summary includes all apostles as wonder workers. Again, Christians gather in Solomon's Portico (NRSV) or *Colonade* (NIV) (see 3:11). The picture is of remarkably powerful Christians held in near-awe by non-Christians. The result is that many converts are added to the Christian movement. Non-Christian Jews are brought to the apostles. Luke expects even the shadow to have healing power (see 19:12). Word about these incredible events spreads quickly.

Preaching and Healing Continue (5:12-16)

Verses 12-16 form a summary of the apostolic church. Great power is not restricted to Peter alone. Power exists within the entire movement.

Miracles and Resistance (5:17-26)

In verses 17-18 resistance to the Christians still comes from the Sadducees. In this second confrontation episode Luke identifies jealousy as the Sadducees' motive (compare this passage to Acts 4:1-31 where resurrection is the issue). Evidently the aristocratic party feels threatened by the mounting popularity of the Christian movement.

The imprisonment provides an opportunity for an angel's intervention. The miraculous release theme is repeated three times in Acts (see 12:6-11 with Peter, 16:25-34 wit Paul and Silas). Ignoring the Sadducees' instruction never to speak Jesus' name again, the apostles immediately go to the Temple to preach.

This life (NRSV) or *new life* (NIV) refers both to Jesus' life and to salvation through Jesus.

An Appearance Before the Council (5:27-32)

The Jewish officials appear very confused and perturbed. Escaped prisoners could cause terrible problems. But the Christians have no intention of creating a disturbance. They intend to preach and teach.

Luke subtly shows that the Christian movement has still not stirred massive resistance. In fact, the Christians seem to have evoked awe among observers. It could have been solely their preaching, which in itself is sufficiently inspiring. However, the apostles' courage and conviction of principles may also have been awe-inspiring to observers. Not many people dared to challenge the High Council (Sanhedrin).

Predictably, the High Priest's charge has to do with the earlier ban on preaching. Now a significant detail of the preaching finds sharp expression. The death of Jesus, central in the kerygma, is lifted up as a particularly important issue. The Jewish officials interpret the preaching as an attempt to blame the Jews for Jesus death (see 4:10). In the earlier preaching, Jesus' death, while not merely incidental, is not emphasized. Here the death of Jesus is described. Surely the Sanhedrin as well as every listener could recall, if not the specific death of Jesus, other deaths equally as repulsive and horrible. Crucifixion was a particularly offensive death.

For a second time Peter refuses to submit to the Sanhedrin. Earlier Peter had raised the issue of authority and had charged the council with the responsibility for making the judgment. Now he becomes more specific. The apostles will not concede to the demands made by the Jewish authorities.

Preaching about Christ's work leads people to repentance and remission of sins. Except for a timely intervention, the apostles might have been killed.

Gamaliel's Wise Counsel (5:33-42)

Luke again indicates that the Christian movement had still not stirred widespread antagonism. In this scene a Pharisee named Gamaliel intervenes. The subtle point Luke makes is that the Pharisees do not yet oppose the Christian movement. Up to this point Christianity is still a relatively small movement within Jewish tradition and life.

Theudas had led an abortive uprising during Procurator Fadus' reign, A.D. 44–46. Technically the event took place later in history than the speech indicates. The point to be noted, however, is that the insight from history is still valid. Action not led by God will fail. Another uprising led by Judas the Galilean suffered a similar fate.

A precarious tension now protects the Christian movement. History has shown utter catastrophe for movements directed by human beings. But God may be working in a new and fresh way. Gamaliel's wise counsel is to trust the verdicts of history rather than run the risk of fighting God.

A beating means flogging thirty-nine strokes (see 2 Corinthians 11:24; Acts 22:19; Mark 13:9). In many instances this punishment could kill a person.

Ignoring both the charge and the beating, the Christians continue their preaching. The apostles will continue to suffer because of the name of Jesus (see 9:16; 15:26; 21:13).

Cracks in the Foundation (6:1-4)

In contrast to the ideal image of the congregation in chapter 4, Luke points here to a sharply divided congregation. The time span in all of the early chapters is unclear. Now in those days serves as both a link and a transition to other material.

Hellenists are Greek-speaking Jews who are from regions throughout the Mediterranean.

Discrimination begins with the economy of the congregation. During this era there were hundreds of religious officials concerned about the traditions of worship, ritual, circumcision, and maintaining separation from the Gentiles. Here the Christian congregation is concerned with serving people as people. Note that the congregation has its own authority to designate these tasks.

Selection of Stephen (6:5-15)

Luke's concern is with Stephen and Philip. They are named first. Both of these men see more readily than the others the implications of the Christian gospel. The message of Jesus cannot be long restricted to the Jewish synagogue and tradition.

The word *convert* (NIV) or *proselyte* (NRSV) is used to refer to a convert to the Jewish faith.

In summary fashion Luke shows how rapidly the Christian movement has grown. Christianity at this time is still within the structures of Judaism. Except for the Sadducees' resistance, no other antagonism has yet developed, either from Judaism or within the Christian movement itself.

Stephen is the first to recognize the implications of Christianity. It must be universal. His insights threaten Hellenistic Jews. With verse 8 Christianity begins the process of transformation from a sect to a worldwide movement.

Freedmen means former slaves, whether they are Jewish or converts.

Stephen's offense is more accurately an encouragement of national and racial pride than it is an actual blasphemy. When words will not silence the threat, violence is the next resort. In order to show Stephen as an ultimate threat to Judaism, the instigators deliberately skew the charges. Luke concludes the chapter picturing Stephen facing an enraged council with serene courage.

§ § § § § § §

The Message of Acts 5–6

These two chapters of Acts present a variety of material. In contrast to the ideal image of chapter 4, in chapters 5 and 6 the images of life within the new movement reveal significant discord and conflict.

Many contemporary Christians labor under the idea that in the early years of the church there was a time when all was perfect. Many express a desire to somehow retrieve this ideal state of a pristine movement. A careful reading of any of the Gospels, however, reveals disagreement and pride among the disciples. Luke's narratives in Acts reveal similar stresses. Conflict seems to characterize the human experience in community. Lies, deceptions, feelings of threat, and mixed motives always exist alongside the possibilities of love, compassion, healing, and influence.

Rather than becoming discouraged because we moderns cannot achieve a long-lost perfection, we can draw comfort and courage from the narratives in Acts. The Christian movement has never been perfect. But God has continually been present with and has led the fallible instruments of apostles and converts.

In a larger sense, Luke uses the internal stresses to mirror the growing resistance and stress developing outside the movement. Through it all, the wise counsel of Gamaliel and the subtle insistence of God shine.

What can we learn from these chapters?

§ We cannot deceive others without deceiving God.
§ The Holy Spirit gives the gift of perception and insight.
§ The presence of the Holy Spirit does not necessarily require spectacular signs and events.

§ Wisdom is also a manifestation of the presence of the Holy spirit.

§ We must never underestimate the influence that an individual may have.

§ Christian witness is expressed in both word and action.

§ God works in fresh and often peculiar ways.

§ Wise counsel sometimes is to refrain from immediate and arbitrary resistance.

§ When argument fails, violence is frequently the next step.

§ Christian witness requires courage since effective preaching usually evokes a response.

§ Sometimes only a minority can initially see the implications of any broad-reaching truth.

§ § § § § § §

Acts 7

Introduction to This Chapter

In this part we will examine the speech and martyrdom of Stephen. Previous confrontations with the High Council—the Sanhedrin—ended first with threats (4:17, 21) and beatings (5:40). This trial will end with a brutal killing. Chapter 7 shows us Stephen's courage in face of anger, a speech filled with accusations, and a screaming mob.

In addition to the vivid narrative, we must keep in mind how Luke uses this dramatic series of events. All along Luke has indicated how the name of Jesus gives life. Proclamation could also stir resistance. The death of Jesus figures highly in this sermon. Clearly Luke draws a similarity between Jesus' death and Stephen's martyrdom.

Here is an outline of chapter 7:
I. Stephen's Speech (7:1-53)
   A. Abraham's Story (7:2-8)
   B. Joseph's Story (7:9-16)
   C. Transition (7:17)
   D. Moses' Story (7:18-43)
   E. Ark of the Covenant (7:44-46)
   F. Polemic Against the Temple (7:47-50)
   G. A Stinging Indictment (7:51-53)
II. Stephen's Death by Stoning (7:54-60)

Stephen's Speech (7:1-53)

Stephen's speech occupies nearly the whole chapter. Throughout the entire presentation the history of the

Jews is retold with a particular emphasis: how the Jews have repeatedly ignored the leading of God and killed the leaders God has lifted up for them.

Abraham's Story (7:2-8)

Luke follows the narrative in Genesis 11:27–12:4. Abraham left Ur after his father's death. No mention is made of the cave at Machpelah near Haran. In the Genesis account Abraham purchased a grave for his wife (see Genesis 23).

Slavery lasted for about 400 years (see the note in Genesis 15:13). Exodus 12:40 gives a more precise figure of 430 years.

Covenant and circumcision are both gifts of grace that come from God. Isaac's circumcision is mentioned (Genesis 21:4). The speech then makes a transition to the Joseph story.

Joseph's Story (7:9-16)

Joseph's brothers' jealousy results in his enslavement (Genesis 37:28). The fact that God was with Joseph will encourage Christians in their current stress. The entire cycle of Joseph stories emphasizes the importance of God's presence with God's chosen people.

Genesis 46:26 indicates that sixty-six people were with Joseph. If we add Joseph's nine sons to this number we arrive at the seventy-five persons mentioned in this sermon.

Shechem is an important Israeliete religious and political center in the hill country of Ephraim (see Joshua 20:7). The location of the grave seems to be confused with Jacob's tomb (see Genesis 33:19; 50:13). The error can be attributed in part to this being a citation from memory and not a printed text.

Transition (7:17)

Luke now makes the transition to the Moses story. The prophecy of 7:6 is fulfilled; the Hebrews are enslaved.

But God still protects them from annihilation. Here Moses is characterized by both deeds and words. In the Exodus account his brother Aaron is the spokesman (see Exodus 4:10-16).

Moses' Story (7:18-43)

The 120 years of Moses' lifetime are sometimes divided into three forty-year periods. He recalls his identity and wishes to visit with his brothers, the slaves. The killing of an abusive Egyptian is interpreted as the will of God. For the first time in this sermon Stephen mentions that the Hebrews did not see the saving person sent by God. Thus, Stephen states the theme of the sermon. The two Hebrew slaves refused to heed Moses' authority. Instead, they mocked him. The implication is, of course, that the Jews have a history of refusing to heed those sent by God.

During the second forty-year period of Moses' life, the voice of God is added to the visual manifestation reported in Exodus 3:3. The entire Moses story crests with God sending him back to Egypt. Mount Sinai is in Arabia, so it is foreign ground.

The Ark of the Covenant (7:44-46)

The intensity of Stephen's argument increases. Evidence is stacked high against the early Israelites. But no one could miss the real import of the message. As the ancient Israelites refused Moses, so the Jews now reject Jesus. Leader and redeemer are rejected. *Living words* (NIV) or *oracles* (NRSV) means the Torah or Law which, broadly translated, means revelation.

As if the previous indictment weren't enough, the analysis continues with yet another incident, this time Aaron's making of the golden idol. Stephen's argument will eventually lead to a condemnation of the Temple. We see here an anticipation of condemnation when the early Israelites worshiped what they made with their own hands.

God gives the people over to idolatry, thus fulfilling the prophecy of Deuteronomy 4:19 (see Amos 5:25-27).

Still, the ancient Israelites did have the tent fortress. The tent gave them a place to represent the presence of God. *Beyond Babylon* in verse 43 refers to the catastrophic Exile.

Verse 45 refers to the ark of the covenant. (See Joshua 3:14; 18:1.)

Polemic Against the Temple (7:47-50)

The Temple that Solomon built was different from the tabernacle. The tabernacle could be moved, thus symbolizing the universal presence of God. The Temple is made more permanent and obviously immovable.

Stephen's speech now takes on a very strong tone. God does not dwell in buildings, such as the Temple. Clearly, Stephen asserts that the building of the Temple is an apostasy.

Verses 49-50 are a direct quote of Isaiah 66:1-2.

A Stinging Indictment (7:51-53)

Allusion to history and implied accusation now give way to a diatribe against those who are stiff-necked and uncircumcised of heart and ear. As if there were any possibility of missing the point, Stephen finally blurts out the scathing indictment. Jews always resist the Holy Spirit, whether it is acting through prophets or through Jesus. They are guilty of a willful blindness to truth and a reactionary anger at anything new and fresh, according to Stephen's speech.

Some questions must be addressed. Does Stephen ever answer the charges that are brought against him? He does not. Some commentators assume this means that Stephen's speech is from another source. Others see the theme, but no direct answer to the indictment. Another possibility is that Luke uses the speech for his own purposes. Luke had seen persecution and death as part of the Christian experience. This speech gives historical precedence to this cruel fact. Luke's experience, and very probably the experience of the congregation(s) he has in mind when writing, is one of endurance under persecution. This angry diatribe against Jews, not just Sadducees, draws a sharp distinction between Christians and Jews.

A latent danger must be identified before proceeding any further. The broad condemnation of Judaism in Stephen's speech has been used far too frequently as fuel for modern anti-semitists. However, the peril of religious people protecting themselves against new truth is not solely a Jewish issue. All religion has the potential of striking hardest at whatever threatens it, Christianity included.

Among the ironies of history are heretics who are kind and compassionate, while the religiously orthodox can be incredibly harsh and unforgiving. Defenders of the faith have shown an alarming inclination toward force and violence. Before modern readers excitedly accuse Jews of shortsightedness, we should understand what Stephen's speech does. The speech reinterprets history. We have all heard of our tradition from well-worn perspectives. But what do we feel when our history is interpreted from the perspective of an outsider? What reactions do we have when oppressed minorities reinterpret history? How do men react when they hear feminist perspectives? Any significant reinterpretation of history and tradition will inevitably lead to disagreement, resistance, and defensiveness. Under stress listeners will not hear subtleties.

Stephen's Death by Stoning (7:54-60)

In the past people shouted for Jesus' crucifixion. Now people scream for Stephen's stoning.

Under extreme duress the Holy Spirit fills Stephen. *Jesus standing at the right hand of God* could imply Jesus anointing Stephen. The image could also mean Jesus standing to receive the messianic office. The image recalls the son of man in Daniel 7:13.

In any event, the mob understands these visions as blasphemy. Nearly in a frenzy already, the crowd is now further enraged. Violence is not far away.

The killing does not occur within the city walls. Luke describes a horrible scene: a stripped man, an enraged mob. With great skill, Luke introduces Saul into the dramatic narrative. The condemned man's clothes are laid at Saul's feet. Stephen kneels, prays, and dies. Recalling Jesus' last words (Luke 23:46), Stephen prays that the crime not be held against the people.

The Christian movement that had begun with miracles and widespread awe now has its first martyr. The Holy Spirit has been present not only during the moments of warmth and success but during extreme duress as well. Christians can take great comfort from this truth.

§ § § § § § §

The Message of Acts 7

Strictly speaking, this chapter is Stephen's polemic against the Jews, especially against the importance of the Temple. Luke uses the speech to show how Christians came under attack. More broadly interpreted, however, Stephen's speech reinterprets history. In his interpretation the Jews repeatedly rejected God's overtures. The peril of a closed faith that attacks when challenged is a Christian one as well.

What learning can we glean from this chapter?

§ God repeatedly attempts to reach toward the creation through prophets and apostles.

§ God calls men and women for special tasks.

§ God is not restricted to national boundaries or buildings. God is everywhere.

§ God is present with the faithful in all circumstances.

§ Any significantly different interpretation of history by a minority will threaten the long-held tradition of the majority.

§ § § § § § §

Acts 8–9

Introduction to These Chapters

In the opening verses of Acts the apostles are told they will be witnesses in Jerusalem, Judea, Samaria and all the world. Through various incidents we have seen how the Christian movement began as a small, relatively obscure sect within Judaism. Increasingly, resistance to the rapidly growing movement mounts. Evidently persecution erupts. In these two chapters the localized movement begins its phenomenal expansion into all the world.

Here is an outline of these chapters:
  I. Persecution and Introduction of Saul (8:1-3)
 II. Philip in Samaria (8:4-8)
III. Simon the Magician (8:9-13)
 IV. Baptism of the Holy Spirit (8:14-25)
  V. Philip and the Ethiopian Eunuch (8:26-40)
 VI. The Conversion of Saul (9:1-31)
      A. On the Road to Damascus (9:1-9)
      B. In Damascus (9:10-22)
      C. Escape to Jerusalem (9:23-31)

Persecution and Introduction of Saul (8:1-3)

Luke introduces one of Christianity's major figures during the bloody killing of Stephen. Not only are garments laid at Saul's feet, but Saul consents to Stephen's death. Immediately a widespread persecution breaks out. Christians are scattered, with the exception of the apostles who remain in Jerusalem. No doubt they are in hiding. Stephen is buried by devout non-Christian Jews since the Christians have scattered.

Saul, a young man in verses 1 and 2, is seen in verse 3 as a vicious persecutor seeking out Christians with an increasing rage (see 26:10).

Since Christians have been driven from the city, Christianity itself could not remain primarily a small sect within Judaism. Recall that conflict had developed with Hellenistic Jews. They now disappear. Persecution is now personified in Saul. He forces people to blaspheme (see 26:11). He is present at the trials and he votes for death.

Luke includes a short summary: Christians who are scattered preach the word. A large part of the book of Acts wrestles with the expansion of Christianity into the Gentile world, especially through Paul's work. But other obscure and anonymous Christians are also instrumental in the spreading of the word. Nowhere can we find a clue as to who first established Christian congregations in the cities of Damascus, Antioch, Ephesus, and Rome itself.

Philip in Samaria (8:4-8)

Philip is the second of the Seven (6:5, see also 21:8). He goes to Samaria (1:8). Samaria is the hilly region of Palestine. After the region was defeated by Assyria in the eighth century B.C., Samaria was populated by captives from Babylon and other foreign lands. Therefore, Samaritans are not full-fledged members of the people of Israel.

Sings and wonders by Philip arouse people's interest. But the signs and wonders are means by which Christian preaching is heard. The misuse of miracles is behind Luke's next story.

Simon the Magician (8:9-13)

A movement that centered on Simon had developed. Some persons even thought of Simon as some kind of god. Luke clearly thinks of him as little more than a wizard.

Philip's preaching centers on God's coming Kingdom and the all-powerful name of Jesus which brings people to be baptized. Even Simon is impressed, and stays to be baptized and see the dramatic events.

Baptism of the Holy Spirit (8:14-25)

The scene shifts suddenly. The apostles, still in Jerusalem, get word of Philip's work. Peter and John are dispatched immediately. Luke minimizes Philip's work by placing the real power, the Holy Spirit, with Peter and John.

The word for purchasing church offices, *simony*, is derived from this event. The Spirit is not for crass human gain. Peter's invective curses Simon severely. The doubt implicit in Peter's comment has to do with Simon's capacity to repent, not whether God has the capacity to forgive.

Gall of bitterness (NRSV) or *full of bitterness* (NIV) is a metaphor for the condition of sin (see Deuteronomy 29:18).

We are left wondering whether the sinsick man's request is answered. The important aspect of the narrative is that Christianity, with its terrific power to offer the Holy Spirit, is far superior to magic and charlatans. Luke will tell of other similar encounters later in Acts (see 13:6-12 and 19:33-41).

Philip and the Ethiopian Eunuch (8:26-40)

In this narrative we see again the Christian mission expanded beyond the confines of Jerusalem. Luke notes that this event does not occur because of human inclination. An angel or spirit directs Philip.

Eunuch frequently means a castrated man. But the term can also mean a high political, court, or military official. *Candace* is the title of the queen of Ethiopia.

Christians very early saw Isaiah 53 referring to Jesus as the suffering servant and saw these servant passages as referring to the passion of Jesus. The Ethiopian must have an interpreter in order to understand Isaiah 53:7-8.

Philip baptizes the man. No details are given. Luke is able to focus primarily on the sheer joy of the event.

In what strikes the modern reader as a peculiar if not impossible event, Philip is transported to Azotus. Philip may have been part of the establishment of Christian congregations in Lydda, Joppa, and Caesarea as he preaches his way to Caesarea, the Roman procurator's headquarters.

Tow aspects of this narrative indicate its importance. The story takes place between the conversion of the Samaritans (in chapter 8) and Gentiles (in chapter 10). Here a Greek works for conversion, serving as a parallel to the upcoming Peter and Cornelius narrative. The event also shows a dependence upon divine intervention and directive.

The Conversion of Saul (9:1-31)

Chapter 9 contains the first of three narratives of Saul's conversion. We will note at the outset that details differ somewhat among the narratives. Despite these small differences, the truth is that something quite remarkable happened. The triple narrative gives strong literary importance to the conversion.

On the Road to Damascus (9:1-9)

Evidently Saul was the driving force behind the persecutions. *The Way* (see 19:9, 23; 22:4; 24:14, 22) also means the saving action of God.

Damascus is a large trading city at the foot of the mountains, in which there is a large Jewish settlement.

Intense light shines on Saul, causing him to fall. (Compare with 22:6 in which the light shines on his companions as well.) Glory to God or Christ sometimes is described as light (see Corinthians 3:18; 4:6).

The dialogue is the same in all three accounts. Whoever persecutes the church persecutes Christ (see Luke 10:16).

Saul, once powerful, is now weak and has to be led. Luke uses these vivid images to illustrate the strength and power of the Spirit and Christ. The rest of the party hears the voice but does not share in the dramatic revelation.

The irony of Saul's condition is very clear. Once he terrorized Christians; now he has to led by the hand. The blindness lasts three days, thus signifying an internal change as well.

In Damascus (9:10-22)

Ananias has exact information. Luke indicates precise direction by the Spirit. The street called *Straight* extends from east to west with gates at each end. This area is modern Darb el-Mostakim.

Vision and prayer are linked (see 10:3, 30; 22:17). Prayer is evidence of an authentic conversion.

The time span of Acts is quite difficult to determine. Ananias has heard Saul, which indicates that a large amount of time has elapsed. Saul previous authority fades in the light of what God has in mind. Saul becomes a chosen instrument (see Romans 9:22-23; 2 Corinthians 4:7).

Verse 16 points out an ironic reversal. Saul had set out to make Christians suffer; now he would suffer as a Christian. Note the sequence: laying on of hands, receiving the Holy Spirit, and then baptism. Thus Saul joins the Christian community and preaches Jesus as the Son of God (see Psalm 2:7; Acts 13:33). The scene ends with the Christians once again increasing in power and influence.

Escape to Jerusalem (9:23-31)

According to Saul's own account, King Aretas is behind the plot spoken of in verses 23-25 (2 Corinthians 11:32-33).

Since Saul returns to Christians in Jerusalem, some Christians had evidently survived the earlier persecutions. Perhaps they had been driven underground and only recently had emerged into public life. Saul later implies that he visits Jerusalem after a period of three years (see Galatians 1:18-20).

Open association with Christians is a tacit confession of faith in Jesus. The apostles approve of Saul.

Debate and attempted conversion are restricted to the Greeks at this point. The Gentile mission will come later.

Tarsus is Saul's home city (see 22:3).

The persecution dies out not only in Jerusalem but throughout Palestine. Christians later understood the end of persecutions to be part of the Holy Spirit's activity. Luke has skillfully shown Saul's conversion and the initial acceptance by the apostles. Saul has now been authorized. Already he has begun debate and preached Jesus as the Son of God.

Luke seems quite unconcerned about how Christian congregations were started in other areas. The real task of the Spirit and the missionaries will be to break down the racial and national boundaries that exist in people's thinking.

§ § § § § § §

The Message of Acts 8–9

In these chapters we have seen Christianity survive a widespread attack. Luke shows not only the broad stroke outline, but a specific man set on destroying the movement. For sheer drama these chapters rank high. The power of the Spirit seen earlier in miracles now manifests itself through the conversion of Christianity's greatest enemy.

What can we learn from these chapters?

§ The Holy Spirit works in subtle ways as well as spectacular ways.

§ The Holy Spirit's power is far superior to mere magic.

§ The power of the Holy Spirit cannot be purchased.

§ The scripture must be interpreted.

§ Christianity yearns to expand itself to other persons and regions.

§ Even the most adamant persecutors can be converted.

§ No power can ultimately resist the power of God.

§ Occasionally Christians will have to trust in the authenticity of conversion and trust formerly detested enemies.

§ Persecution has its hour, but God's intention always prevails.

§ § § § § § §

Acts 10

Introduction to This Chapter

In the last section we concluded with Saul's return to
Jerusalem and the ending to a wave of persecution. This
part begins a new section in which Peter extends the
Christian movement to the Gentiles. Previously,
Christianity had transcended traditional boundaries of
contempt (Samaritans) and legal barriers (a eunuch could
not be a Jew). Now the movement begins to reach far
beyond even the apostles' imagination.

Here is an outline of Acts 9:32–10:48:
  I. Peter at Lydda (9:32-35)
 II. Peter at Joppa (9:36-43)
III. The Vision of Cornelius (10:1-8)
 IV. Peter's Vision (10:9-16)
  V. The Envoy's Journey (10:17-23)
 VI. Peter Goes to Caesarea (10:24-33)
VII. Peter's Speech (10:34-43)
VIII. The Results of Preaching (10:44-48)

Peter at Lydda (9:32-35)
Lydda is in the plain of Sharon. It is located at
present-day Ludd, about twenty-five miles northwest of
Jerusalem. The Hebrews often spoke of Jerusalem as a
height. Thus any journey away from Jerusalem is down.
As in earlier miracles, the name of Jesus has remarkable
power. The scene is reminiscent of Jesus' healing of the

lame man, after which he instructs the man to take up his bed and walk.

The people are Jews. Luke has not yet shown that Christianity expanded to the Gentiles.

Peter at Joppa (9:36-43)

An abrupt transition changes the scene to Joppa, modern-day Jaffa. *Dorcas* means *gazelle* in Greek.

The miracle follows the Hebrew tradition in which the afflicted person is taken to a better ventilated room (1 Kings 17:17-24). Dorcas' works are shown to illustrate what sort of person she is, not in order to purchase the divine healing.

Note that the name of Jesus is not mentioned in verses 40-41. The story is similar to Jesus' healing in Mark 5:40.

Predictably, Jews in the area are brought into the Christian faith. With a series of short narratives, Luke has shown Christianity being established in Judea, Samaria, and Galilee. When reading Acts we must keep in mind Luke's various purposes. One is to show the expansion of the Christian movement throughout the Mediterranean all the way to Rome. And such expansion in turn shows the remarkable power of Christ and the Holy Spirit. Luke has no need to explain how each and every congregation is established. Here he uses vignettes to represent widespread phenomena.

The Vision of Cornelius (10:1-8)

In previous encounters Christianity met with resistance from Sadducees and some other Jews. In this chapter Luke begins illustrating the resistance to expansion that comes from within the Christian community itself.

Caesarea is an excellent harbor. The city is the seat of the Roman proconsul. A garrison of Roman troops is stationed here. A centurion is a man who has risen through the ranks with one hundred men under his command. A cohort numbers six hundred men.

Cornelius is described as a pious man. Gentiles who took part in Jewish services are called *God-fearers,* similar to the Ethiopian eunuch. They were not pagans like the jailkeeper we will see in Philippi.

Luke graciously shows the Gentile in the initial scene. Clearly the Holy Spirit is at work. This development is the intention of God. Peter's reluctance will appear all the more sharply against the openness of the Gentile, Cornelius.

Cornelius is ignorant of Peter's identity, evidence again of the Holy Spirit's leading. Men are dispatched to Joppa. The importance of 9:43 is now apparent.

Peter's Vision (10:9-16)

Peter sees a peculiar collection of animals. All these animals are, for various reasons, according to tradition, not to be eaten. *Impure* (NIV) or *profane* (NRSV) or unclean is a way of stating emphasis in the Hebrew language. This device is called a *hendiadys.*

Three refusals add emphasis. The Spirit, however, will not be stayed. Peter contradicts what Jesus had said earlier (see Mark 7:15).

The Envoy's Journey (10:17-23)

Peter, still perplexed, receives visitors. The vision is not yet explained. A recapitulation of previous events emphasizes the fact that the Holy Spirit directs the entire series of episodes. The Roman centurion is described in favorable terms. Luke also portrays a centurion favorably in his Gospel (see Luke 7:1-10 and 23:47).

Peter recovers sufficiently to play a somewhat confused but gracious host. Luke cleverly shows how the Christians did not voluntarily grasp the significance of earlier implications (1:8). Had it not been for the Spirit, the expansion would have ended early.

The reluctant participant journeys to Caesarea. Jonah had tried to flee to Joppa but ended up reluctantly going to Nineveh. Peter must leave Joppa as well to continue God's mission.

Peter Goes to Caesarea (10:24-33)

A holy Angel (verse 22) implies the same authority as the Spirit. God has prepared a congregation for Peter. In another incident, human agents for God's purposes are presumed to be gods. Peter refuses to accept this treatment.

The meaning of the vision is finally clear. People, not foods, are the focus of God's concern. God has been guiding the entire unprecedented series of events. Previously Peter has been requested to perform a miraculous healing.

Cornelius describes his remarkable vision. Luke presents a God-fearer who wants to hear more. We might even suggest that it was not so much Peter opening the door to Christianity as it was the Gentiles opening the door for Peter. By implication, then, the Gentiles were opening the door for true Christians with similarly restricted perspectives on the Christian movement and message.

Peter's Speech (10:34-43)

Peter gives a lengthy sermon that contains many of the elements of the kerygma. He begins with an astonishing insight toward which the Holy Spirit has been laboring since the outset. God does not discriminate with respect to which persons may be admitted to Christian salvation. No racial barriers should prevent Christian salvation.

Readers must make certain they understand the difference between the manifestations of the Spirit at Pentecost and at Caesarea. During Pentecost, other Jews heard their own native language. Men and women had gathered from all around the Mediterranean. A large number of different languages would not be uncommon.

The action of the Spirit in that setting was to transpose the babble into language intelligible to the hearer. Luke makes it quite clear that each person heard in a legitimate language. At Caesarea, on the other hand, the congregation is overwhelmed by the power of the Holy Spirit. The people erupt into ecstatic, or pneumatic, speech. The technical name for this kind of utterance is *glossalalia*.

Peter raises a rhetorical question regarding the limits of baptism. Clearly the message of the entire drama has been that God wants no restrictions on Christian fellowship. However, Christianity will resist the implications of this keen insight, sometimes quite vociferously (see 10:14, 28; 11:2, 8, 17). Luke is obviously speaking to the readers of his work through this question. Note that Peter himself does not baptize. The converts are baptized in the name of Jesus Christ; the trinitarian formula is not used.

The Results of Preaching (10:44-48)

Luke's purpose throughout the drama is to show that God introduced Gentiles into the church. The authority and validity of the Gentile mission did not rest upon the imaginations and decisions of human beings, even if they are apostles. The expansion of Christianity beyond traditional boundaries of race, religion, and nation is God's intention. The apostles are led by no less an authority than the Holy Spirit. Luke drives home this point by showing Peter, and later others, both hesitant and confused by the divine imperative.

A more subtle and perhaps lesser concern is also addressed in these verses. By showing the Roman to be a good man (as in his Gospel), Luke implies good relationships between the Christian movement and Roman authority. Such cooperation would secure tolerance for Christians.

§ § § § § § §

The Message of Acts 10

Saul's conversion through Peter's mission to Cornelius in Caesarea affords many insights into the purposes of God.

What can we learn from these chapters?

§ As with Saul, wrong actions can be taken for the right reasons.

§ Conversion of even the most adamant is possible.

§ The Christian witness frequently requires courage.

§ The Holy Spirit will supply courage sufficient to the task and the hour.

§ God leads people to fresh and exciting insights.

§ God wants no barriers because of race, religion, or nation.

§ People of different traditions, races, or national origins are all God's people.

§ Preaching can be a very powerful enterprise.

§ § § § § § §

Acts 11–12

Introduction to These Chapters

Peter's startling insight opens enormous possibilities for the spread of Christianity. However, the expansion of the movement is by no means without hindrance. God's intention will have to struggle mightily against external powers as well as internal dissension and resistance. In these two chapters the Christian mission takes deeper roots in Antioch. This firm foundation will be critical when storms of persecution break against Christianity.

Here is an outline of Acts 11 and 12
   I. Against the Gentile Mission (11:1-17)
  II. The Brethren Are Silenced (11:18)
 III. A Mission to the Greeks (11:19-26)
  IV. Christian Famine Relief (11:27-30)
   V. Herod Agrippa's Persecution Begins (12:1-4)
  VI. A Miraculous Escape for Peter (12:5-19)
 VII. The Death of Herod Agrippa (12:20-23)
VIII. Paul's First Missionary Journey (12:24-25)

Against the Gentile Mission (11:1-17)

The shock of Peter's insight and the subsequent baptisms is nearly impossible for modern readers to realize. It is sufficient to say that the news of his radical departure from tradition reaches Jerusalem long before he arrives.

Up to Jerusalem refers to the elevation of the city; one

always goes *up* to Jerusalem. When Peter arrives in Jerusalem, the conservatives await him. Not only is baptism a concern for these people, but the custom of sharing meals as well. The extent to which Christianity has already exceeded tradition is critical. First Jews and converts were attracted to and included in the movement. Next the Samaritans were included (see 8:14). *God-fearers*, Gentiles who attended worship services and practiced their piety (such as the Italian centurion), were the next major group that Christianity embraced. Whether or not the conservative faction felt uncomfortable with these groups we cannot determine. But this chapter offers stark evidence that the Gentiles have not yet been accepted into the fold.

Peter's self-defense is not a mere repetition of the preceding events. Some differences in detail do occur. In verse 11, six Jewish Christians are already with him at his house. In verse 14, the angels reveal to Cornelius what Peter will say. In verse 15, the Spirit comes as Peter begins preaching. In verse 16, Peter remembers the words of Jesus. These differences in detail do not take away from the truth of this remarkable event. God is clearly at work. Luke seems to be stressing this point throughout these early chapters. Repeatedly, the emphasis is on the work of God and the Holy Spirit.

In ringing conclusion Peter asks two penetrating questions. Clearly Luke intends to pose these same questions to his readers as well. Since the same Spirit is given to new converts as had been bestowed upon apostles, who is Peter (or any individual for that matter) to resist God? How can an individual prevent God's intentions from their accomplishment? The wisdom is reminiscent of Gamaliel's counsel (see 5:34-39).

The Brethren Are Silenced (11:18)

The identity of the opponents in the conservative party is unknown. Could they have been the other eleven apostles? Perhaps, but this may have been just too shocking to be put into print. The important fact is not the identity of specific opponents. What Luke illustrates is that what may have begun as an isolated event has now become a matter of general principle in the Christian church.

A Mission to the Greeks (11:19-26)

God uses the scattered Christians to establish new congregations. Here Luke picks up the theme of Acts 8:1. Phoenicia is a coastal strip of territory about seventy-five miles long and seven and one-half miles wide at its widest point. It extends from Cape Carmel north to the Elentheros River. Antioch, on the Orontes river about twenty miles inland, with its population of some one-half million, is the third largest city in the Roman empire. As yet, these scattered Christians do not generally speak to Gentiles.

Barnabas is from Cyprus (see 4:36). Some of the Christians preach to Greeks, that is, Gentiles, without reference to circumcision. Evidently the insight Peter had earlier comes to other Christians as well.

The remarkable growth of the Christian movement is sufficient evidence to show that the enterprise really does belong to God. *The hand of the Lord* (NRSV) or *the Lord's hand* (NIV) is also referred to in 13:11.

Once again, the news of Christians transcending traditional barriers reaches Jerusalem. Barnabas emerges as representative of the Jerusalem congregation. His authority may stem from his exemplary action (see 4:36-37). He will be first on the list of prophets and teachers in Antioch (see 13:1). In any event, he is described as a good man, full of the Holy Spirit and of faith. (Compare this description with Luke 23:50 regarding Joseph of Arimathea, and with Acts 6:5 regarding Stephen). Barnabas will accompany Paul on the missionary journey. Barnabas may therefore have been sent to validate the Christian outreach to the Gentiles.

The presence of the Holy spirit authenticates the mission.

Luke assumes that Paul remains in Tarsus (see 9:30). In Paul's life a year's stay is quite a long time.

The term *Christian* used to describe the new movement is a very important detail. Up to this point, Christianity has been a sect, albeit a very active one, within Judaism. Using the term *Christian* here accomplishes two ends. First, the movement assumes its own identity. Second, Christianity cannot expect protection by the Roman government. When Christianity takes on its own identity, Christians must wrestle with the problem of continuing their deep rootage in the Judaic past and tradition.

Christian Famine Relief (11:27-30)

At this time is impossible to date precisely, as with most of the event in Acts. Famine did occur in the years A.D. 41–54. However, that famine was not universal.

A different collection is mentioned numerous times in Paul's letters (see 1 Corinthians 16:15; 2 Corinthians 8:4; 9:1, 13; and Romans 15:31).

Luke assumes the office of *elder*. We have no indication of how the office came into being. Here the elders perform supervisory duties. They may parallel the Seven.

What is Luke's purpose in this short narrative? To begin with, he shows the relationship between the two congregations in Jerusalem and Antioch. Evidently the Antiochan congregation has already developed its own missionary effort that is independent from the Jerusalem church (see 15:23).

Herod Agrippa's Persecution Begins (12:1-4)

A new wave of persecution erupts under Herod Agrippa (born in 10 B.C.; died in A.D. 44), the grandson of

Herod the Great. The terse narrative suggests summary executions.

Up to this time Christians are tolerated, if not accepted, by a majority of Jews, with only Sadducees remaining hostile. Luke makes no distinction now. *During the feast* (NIV) or *festival of Unleavened Bread* (NRSV) identifies Peter's story with Jesus' passion (see Luke 22:1).

A Miraculous Escape for Peter (12:5-19)

Peter's predicament is quite serious. He will be executed on the next day (see John 19:4-8, 13-16). Luke sets the stage for a miracle. Direct intervention comes through an angel. Peter has no part in the escape. The angel even has to instruct Peter how to get dressed. Not until he passes through the prison doors does Peter grasp the reality of his miraculous release. The Lord has rescued Peter from the jaws of death. The congregations' prayers have been heard (see 1:10).

Luke employs humor to show the miraculous nature of this episode. The young girl is so overwhelmed with joy she ignores the escaped fugitive standing in the street. He is left to continue knocking at the door, thus running the risk of arousing suspicion. Realizing how precarious his present circumstances are, Peter motions for quiet. He then leaves, bringing the story to a conclusion.

The next scene is the following day. In events that almost parallel events in chapter 5, the antagonists are shown to be utterly hopeless. Without a prisoner the soldiers are doomed. Whoever contradicts God's intention may have to suffer consequences.

The Death of Herod Agrippa (12:20-23)

Verse 20 seems abrupt. Perhaps it suggests an economic reprisal. Luke matter-of-factly continues with a narrative of Herod's death. As with the soldiers, death seems part of the result of attacking God's intention. An angel of the Lord smites Herod. *Eaten by worms* is a typical description of how persecutors of the church ended up.

Paul's First Missionary Journey (12:24-25)

Against the backdrop of persecution Luke has not only pictured a miraculous rescue, he has also shown how God protects and sustains the Christian movement.

The point could not be lost on Luke's readers. Peter's rescue had nothing to do with Peter's initiative. The entire event is God's own doing. Yes, the Christian congregations pray earnestly. But even when Peter arrives at the front door in the darkness of night, at least one of their number cannot believe that prayer has achieved anything.

In the midst of this glorious story one event casts its shadow. Though Peter survives, James does not. Persecution will inevitably claim some victims. God's protection is not a universal and absolute protection. Luke makes no attempt at explaining why James dies and Peter is rescued. Explanations of this sort try to say more than he knows. Luke shows an appropriate reserve. The fact is that both the cross and God's protection are part of the Christian experience.

Luke's conclusion indicates that while some may suffer and die, the Christian movement does and will prevail.

John Mark enters the narrative. He will accompany Paul and Barnabas to Perga (see 12:25–13:13). Luke then concludes this stirring episode with preparations for the momentous first missionary journey.

§ § § § § § §

The Message of Acts 11–12

What can we learn about God and God's intention from these chapters?

§ Christianity will always yearn to transcend barriers.

§ Initially God's intention may be apparent to only a minority.

§ Resistance to God comes not only from without but from within as well.

§ Congregations develop as a result of anonymous and obscure people as well as famous and well-known people.

§ Christian congregations are related in the mission of God.

§ Christians share from their resources to help others.

§ Christian witness may involve real risk.

§ God protects and sustains the Christian movement and mission.

§ § § § § § §

Acts 13

Introduction to This Chapter

In all the preceding chapters Luke has skillfully woven together many pieces from the earliest years of the new Christian movement. We have noted how he uses specific incidents to illustrate a more widespread phenomenon. Beginning with chapter 13, Luke's narrative becomes a description of the mission of Christianity to the Gentiles. Resistance will inevitably develop both from within the Christian church itself and from the external forces of threatened Jewish elements.

Here is an outline of Acts 13:
I. Barnabas and Saul Called to Mission (13:1-5)
II. Encounter with a Magician (13:6-15)
III. Paul's Sermon (13:16-41)
IV. Trouble Brewing (13:42-47)
V. The Mission Continues (13:48-52)

Barnabas and Saul Called to Mission (13:1-5)

The missionary impulse begins in Antioch. Luke has shown the relationship between the Jerusalem and Antioch congregations. However, the impulse for mission to the Gentiles emerges from the northern congregation. Was it because the Jerusalem conservatives controlled the congregation? We will see in subsequent chapters how the Jerusalem church resists the entire idea of expansion.

Barnabas is well known, as is Saul. Symeon and Lucius are unknown except by name. Manaen is evidently an intimate friend of Herod Antipas. Prophets and teachers are very important in the early church (see Romans 12:6-8; 1 Corinthians 12:28-30; 14:26, 29; Ephesians 4:11).

Luke succinctly portrays two scenes. The first is the selection of the missionaries. The men are selected by the Holy Spirit. In the second scene the missionaries prepare through prayer and fasting. For Luke and the entire church the Holy Spirit's leading is crucial.

Encounter with a Magician (13:6-15)

Seleucia is the harbor city sixteen miles west of Antioch, founded by Seleucius Nicator in about 300 B.C. Solamis is the largest city on Cyprus. Paphos is the capital on the west side of the island.

On Cyprus, Christianity encounters another magician. Bar-Jesus (son of Jesus/Joshua) has real powers. Luke's purpose with this story is to show how Christianity is far superior to mere magical power, since magic essentially opposes God. Therefore, the man is called a false prophet (see Matthew 7:15; 24:11, 24; Luke 6:26; 2 Peter 2:1; 1 John 4:1).

Sergius Paulus is the Roman governor of the island. By showing the Roman to be interested in Christianity, Luke underscores how little threat Christianity poses to Roman authority.

Saul is a Jewish name; Paul is a Roman name. Because Paul had been thoroughly Jewish, his Hebrew name was used. He will now be working with Greeks and Gentiles, so he needs a Roman name. Paul performs the miracle and becomes the leader of the group. The miracle moves the proconsul to faith, in an actual conversion (see John 4:50, 53). Thus Paul's work begins with no less than one of Rome's highest officials. Luke also shows the sharp distinction between magic and Christianity.

From the west coast of Cyprus the journey continues

into Asia Minor (present-day Turkey). *Pamphylia* means *region of all tribes*. Perga is in a poor region between the coast and Mount Taurus.

Luke gives no explanation for John's departure, but there are two possible reasons for Mark's abrupt departure. One tradition is that he was quite young and wanted to be with his mother. Another tradition suggests that he could not tolerate the replacement of Paul for Barnabas as leader of the mission. We will meet Mark again. In the later episode Barnabas and Paul will disagree over the young man's participation in mission. This same Mark may well be the one to whom Paul makes reference in 2 Timothy 4:11.

Antioch in Pisidia, about 100 miles north of Perga, was founded by Seleucius Nicator.

Synagogue services include the *Shema—Hear, O Hear Israel, the Lord your God is one God*; prayers; blessings; readings from the Law (Torah) and the Prophets; and benediction. Anyone could then speak after the reading from the Prophets (see Luke 4:20-27 in which Jesus speaks after the reading of Isaiah).

Paul's Sermon (13:16-41)

This is Paul's first major address. Not surprisingly, the address is a summary of Israel's history (see Stephen's speech in Acts 7:2-53).

The sermon has three distinct section. Verses 17-25 deal with God's preparation for the new message. Verses 26-37 address the new gospel message. Verses 38-41 include the kerygma's call for repentance.

Paul's audience consists of Jews and God-fearers. The patriarchs (Abraham, Isaac, Jacob, and Joseph) are not mentioned, nor is Moses. Already Paul's tone sounds different. His overview of history will not be a thorough and scathing indictment of Jews.

The *seven nations* (see Deuteronomy 7:1) are Hittites, Girgashites, Amorites, Canaanites, Perizzites, Hivites, and Jebusites. According to rabbinic estimates, about 450 years elapsed between the entry into Canaan and the building of the Temple.

The reference in verse 21 is to Saul the king. It is not an autobiographical note.

Paul's use of scripture is typical of kerygmatic interpretation. In this instance two verses are brought together to make one (see 1 Samuel 15:23; 16:12). Jesus fulfills the Old Testament promise of David's son being Israel's savior (see 5:31).

John's baptism is again characterized by repentance. No mention is made either of Jesus' baptism or the baptism of the Holy Spirit (see 10:37-38).

Sects had sprung up that centered on John the Baptist. Paul stresses the Baptist's refusal to assume messiahship. (See also Matthew 3:11; Mark 1:7; Luke 3:15; John 1:19.)

The death of Jesus is central in the kerygma, as evidenced by Peter, Paul, and, by implication, Luke as well. The preaching emphasizes Jesus' innocence also (see Luke 23:4; Acts 3:13). Luke takes great care to show Pilate, and therefore Roman authority, not voluntarily participating in the crucifixion. Paul compresses the Passion into a few succinct words. Note the reference to particularly repulsive death in Jewish tradition, impalement on the tree.

Jesus' resurrection receives special attention. The Resurrection is a fact (3:15; 4:10) attested to by apostolic witness (see also 1 Corinthians 15:4-8). Three major emphases form the apostolic witness: (1) Jesus is risen; (2) Old Testament promises are therefore fulfilled; and (3) this Resurrection is the heart of the message. Unlike mortals, Jesus did not know *corruption* (NRSV; NIV = *decay*). That is, his body did not go the way of all flesh. Scripture is always used to interpret present events (see Psalm 16:10)

Paul builds to the climax of the sermon by drawing a clear distinction between David and Jesus. David's significance pales in comparison to Jesus' importance. Jesus' life is imperishable.

Finally Paul arrives at the crux of his message with its theological importance. Through Jesus we know the remission of sins. Paul generally uses the term *justification* is his letters. Forgiveness is the gift of grace (see 2:38; 5:31; 10:43; 26:18). In conclusion Paul cites Habakkuk 1:5, which states that God will do an unexpected work. Luke is, of course, anticipating the imminent mission to the Gentiles.

Unlike Stephen's speech, which evoked a howling rage, Paul's sermon appeals to the audience. Indeed, the people want more preaching by both Paul and Barnabas in another week.

Trouble Brewing (13:42-47)

Luke now presents Paul as a great speaker, since nearly the entire population turns out to hear him on the subsequent Sabbath. But the massive turnout threatens the Jews. Evidently they very quickly see the beginnings of an independent congregation.

Since Jews have excluded themselves from accepting the message of Salvation, the mission to the Gentiles now finds open expression. For the moment, however, the outreach is restricted to Antioch (see 14:1; 16:13; 17:1, 10, 17; 18:4-6; 19:8; 28:26-28). With the exception of Sergius Paulus (13:7), nothing has been said of a Gentile mission. Paul will continue addressing Jews first, as he will in Corinth (see 18:6). Scripture is again cited as the foundation for the new undertaking. Paul uses the prophet Isaiah as a basis for his work in much the same manner as Luke uses Isaiah for Jesus' work in the Gospel (see Isaiah 49:6; Luke 2:32).

The Mission Continues (13:48-52)

Luke suggests that not only these specific Gentiles but the entire population rejoices at the sharing in the

Resurrection. Evidently the message spreads throughout the area without the need of apostles' presence. Luke has repeatedly implied spontaneity of the gospel throughout these early incidents. Obscure and anonymous people are responsible for the remarkable spreading of the Christian message.

Predictably, the established Jewish congregations feel threatened by the surging Christian movement. Earlier specific theological assertions evoked resistance. Recall the Sadducees' argument against the Resurrection. Paul does not indict Jews for their refusal to accept the Holy Spirit, as Stephen had. In Antioch no mention is made of specific theological tenets. The entire message of the life in Christ becomes the target. Opponents stir popular outcry by using men and women who are leaders in the area. A conspiracy develops which forces the missionaries out.

Luke employs the image Jesus uses (Luke 9:5; 10:11). The men shake the dust from their heels, which showed that the missionaries had completed their duty. One very important point has been made, however. Even though the missionaries depart, a Christian community has been established.

The same anonymous Christians will be visited on the return leg of the journey (see 14:21). Luke again subtly illustrates the stubborn resolve of the Holy Spirit to lead and sustain the Christian enterprise. The communities do not depend simply upon individuals for their survival. Surely Luke's readers would draw great courage from this very simple truth.

Iconium is about eighty miles east of Antioch in a plains region.

Luke brings the Pisidian Antioch episode to a close by once again calling attention to the Holy Spirit (see also 1 Thessalonians 1:6). Preaching and Christian witness has birthed a Christian congregation.

§ § § § § § §

The Message of Acts 13

The first missionary journey begins the great drama of Christianity's expansion to the Gentiles. Along the way Christianity encounters a magician, conspiracy, and hostility. This chapter is bracketed by the Holy Spirit. The Spirit sends the missionaries out, and, at the conclusion, fills them with elation and courage. A more subtle point is that Christianity attracts both critical thinkers and Roman authorities.

What can we learn about God and God's will from this chapter?

§ The Holy Spirit stirs churches and individuals to mission.

§ Prophets and teachers, uniquely gifted people, are used by God in the congregation.

§ New mission and direction require adequate preparation through prayer.

§ Christianity is far superior to charlatans and magicians.

§ Preaching is a foundation for congregations.

§ The power of God's intention overcomes even death. The power of the Resurrection is central to any Christian proclamation.

§ God can and does work through obscure and nameless individuals to sustain congregations.

§ § § § § § §

Introduction to This Chapter

Chapter 13 concluded with the disciples departing from Pisidian Antioch. They were being threatened by an angry populace and filled with the Holy Spirit. The peculiar juxtaposition of threat and Holy Spirit seems both ironic and appropriate. Luke has cleverly described the mixture of feelings that will occur in the Christian mission. He has hinted at suffering and glory, at the cross and the Resurrection. In the balance of this first journey the same ironies and combination of threat and promise continue.

Here is an outline of chapter 14:
 I. A Plot Develops (14:1-5)
 II. The Disciples Flee (14:6-7)
 III. A Cripple Is Healed (14:8-14)
 IV. Paul's Protest (14:15-18)
 V. Return to Antioch (14:19-28)

A Plot Develops (14:1-5)

Iconium is in the Roman province of Galatia in south-central Asia. Paul initiates the Christian work within the synagogue. However, his audience is not restricted solely to Jews. Others attend the services as well, including Gentiles (Greeks). Preaching again evokes belief, which in turns stirs trouble. The threatened element in the synagogue intends to prevent conversions to Christianity (see 17:5, 13). Unlike previous incidents, this resistance seems to stiffen the missionaries' resolve to remain in the city (see 15:35). The missionaries trust in the sufficiency of God (see 9:27-31; 14:3; 18:26; 19:8; 26:26).

Luke describes Paul and Barnabas with the same phrase that was used to describe the Twelve (Acts 5:12). He identifies them both as apostles. The city seethes and is sharply divided.

The Disciples Flee (14:6-7)

Eventually the stress erupts. Jew and non-Jew alike, along with some authorities, conspire against the disciples. The image is one of a narrow escape. Though harried, the missionaries begin preaching immediately upon arrival in Lystra and Derbe.

The entire Iconian episode poses problems for the interpreter. Unlike other travel narratives, no first convert is mentioned. Not only this, but verses 2 and 3 seem to oppose each other. Can we assume that in this city resistance evokes deliberate defiance of the disrupter?

Certainly Luke's purposes are served by these peculiar events. The power of God is seen through preaching and conversions. Bearing witness to the Christian message frequently involves stress and suffering. Moreover, persecution does not achieve its aim of defeating the movement. Persecution sows the seed of another congregation. The narrative also serves as a means by which to link Paul's work in Pisidian Antioch with the dramatic events that will take place in Lystra. Lystra is a Roman colony, modern-day Hatun-Serai, about thirty miles from Iconium.

A Cripple Is Healed (14:8-14)

The threefold description of the lame man emphasizes the severity of his plight (recall Acts 3:2). The exchange does not take place in a synagogue. The man's faith is critical to the prospect of healing (see Mark 9:23; Luke

5:20; 7:50; 8:48; 17:19; 18:42; Acts 3:16). Paul does not speak in the name of Jesus, but extraordinary power still manifests itself.

Speaking in Lycaonian means the people used their peculiar local dialect or vernacular. Their outburst refers to a local legend of Philemon and Baucis, who had entertained Zeus and Hermes. Here they identify Paul as Hermes and Barnabas as Zeus. The priest does not intend to kill Paul and Barnabas, but the missionaries are horrified by the pagan expression.

Paul's Protest (14:15-18)

Paul refuses to allow himself to be the center of attraction and worship (see Galatians 1:8; 4:14; Acts 17:22-31). Paul then attempts to interpret the actions of God in the blatantly pagan populace. Though no specific revelation had been given to them, still God worked on their behalf (see Psalms 145:16; 147:8-9; Isaiah 45:1-6).

Even with the disclaimer the apostles barely restrain the people.

For the first time Luke portrays Christianity coming into contact with a purely pagan environment. In previous encounters some preparation is assumed, either through the traditions of Judaism, the synagogue, or general knowledge and tacit acceptance by the God-fearers. Under these conditions Paul attempts to shift the pagan preoccupation with myth and idols to the living biblical God who created the heavens and the earth and who orders the seasons. At no time during the entire episode is the name of Jesus mentioned. Without some sort of prior preparation the significance of the name will be lost. Here Paul begins that critical preparation. Clearly, Christianity's encounter with pagan cultures will be an awkward one.

Return to Antioch (14:19-28)

A new scene opens in which the inevitable resistance emerges. Evidently new of the recently escaped missionaries filters back to both Antioch and Iconium. Jews, still angry, stir up public opinion against the apostles. Paul refers to this incident in 2 Corinthians 11:25 (see also 2 Timothy 3:11).

Luke uses the beating and Paul's revival to illustrate how the power of the apostles and Christianity are far more important than the sufferings they endure. Derbe is the only place where Paul does not meet with hostility.

Preaching continues to be the central task in the missionaries' work. Though the time period is very difficult to determine, quite a time lapse occurs between the expulsion (14:5) and the missionaries' return trip. One subtle observation is suggested by the short narrative. Christian congregations survived in each of the towns through which the missionaries traveled and from which they had fled.

Luke alludes not only to missionaries' tribulations, but to suffering in the congregations as well. Death is an entry into the kingdom of God (see Luke 16:19-22; 23:43).

An official ecclesiastical hierarchy seems to have been implemented by this time. Elders run the church (see Titus 1:5). Prayers and fasting are significant in the ongoing work of the church.

The return journey receives only the incidental comment that preaching occurs in Perga. No results from this preaching are mentioned. Attalia is the port city founded by King Attalos II of Pergamum (178–159 B.C.).

Luke concludes the first journey by again calling attention to the fact that the entire undertaking is at the direction of the Holy Spirit. The mission is not the result of human initiative. Since Luke stresses the action of the Holy Spirit and God's initiative, the significance of the narrative is not primarily with Paul and Barnabas.

God has allowed Gentiles access to the gift of salvation. A long time elapses between the apostles' return and the opening of the Jerusalem Conference.

The Message of Acts 14

Luke's presentation of the first journey provides many insights into God's intention and the Christian missionary enterprise. Throughout the narrative there is a tension between Christianity's power and Christianity's suffering. Theologically these two perspectives may be called a theology of glory and a theology of the cross. Sensitive Christians have always recognized the necessary relationship between the two. Certainly Luke keeps the tension in balance. To stress one over the other is to run the risk of a truncated gospel. The church must always recognize the glory of God's victory and the suffering of bearing Christ's cross.

What other insights may we glean from this chapter?

§ God is always present with Christians, both in victory and in trial.

§ Christian preaching will evoke response. The word will never go forth to return empty (see Isaiah 55:11).

§ Christian witness will always require courage.

Persecution never achieves its intention. New congregations will be formed.

§ Christians must learn how to speak to a culture not familiar with biblical narrative and revelation.

§ The victory God intends in the Resurrection overshadows suffering (see Romans 8:28, 31-39).

§ God's work continues not only through well-known persons, but through anonymous and obscure persons as well.

§ § § § § § §

First Missionary Journey

From Seleucia to Cyprus (13:4)
  Salamis (13:5)
  Paphos (13:6)

To the coastal region of Pamphylia (13:13)
  Perga (13:13)

Pisidian Antioch (13:14-50)

Iconium (13:51)

Region of Lycaonia (14:6)
  Lystra (14:6)
  Derbe (14:6)

Return through
  Lystra (14:21)
  Iconium (14:21)
  Pisidian Antioch (14:24)
  Pamphylia (14:24)
  Perga (14:25)
  Attalia (14:25)
  Antioch in Syria (14:26)

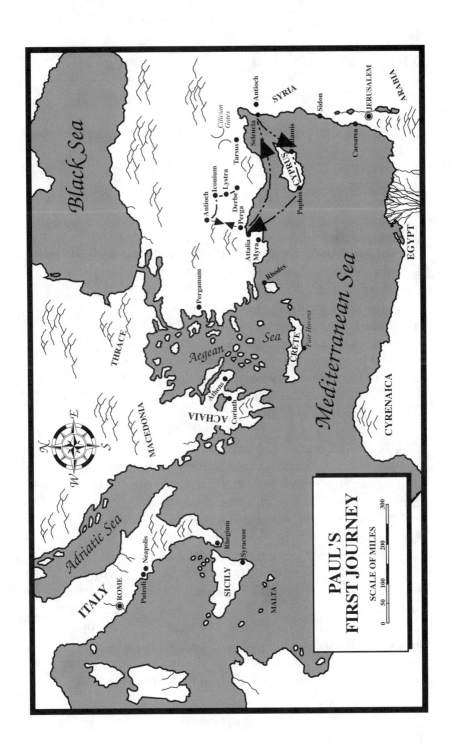

PAUL'S
FIRST JOURNEY

SCALE OF MILES

0   50   100   200   300

Acts 15

Introduction to This Chapter

Chapter 15 is the watershed chapter in Acts.
Throughout the previous chapters Luke has skillfully
illustrated the grand and subtle forces at work in the
Christian movement. The Holy Spirit's presence as
initiative and strength is one of the most important forces
at work. The Holy Spirit is always able to overcome the
external resistance to the mission to the Gentiles.

Christianity begins as a small cadre of disciples within
the structures and traditions of Judaism. Very soon,
however, individuals begin to grasp the vast implications
of Christianity's message.

First Jews, then Samaritans, then God-fearers, then
finally Gentiles who have absolutely no Jewish training
or exposure are attracted to the new movement. The
conservative elements in the Christian church resist this
far-reaching mission. The maintenance of Jewish
tradition seems as important as the celebration of a new
Christian faith.

In this chapter Luke describes the conference in which
the issue of the Gentile mission will be resolved. The
single subject over which the conflict is waged is the
practice of circumcision. The Old Testament tradition
insists upon circumcision. The insight of Christianity is,
in part at least, that this physical event is not necessary
for salvation. In all probability, the hesitation regarding a
mission to the Gentiles, who had no Jewish tradition, is

far more complex than this one apparent cause. Eating with Gentiles, social relations, and cultural differences are all much more difficult to pinpoint.

Luke portrays the Jerusalem Conference in five separate scenes.

Here is an outline of this chapter:

The Jerusalem Conference (15:1-35)

The conservative element is identified as arriving in Antioch from somewhere in Judea, not necessarily from the city of Jerusalem, after the first journey. The controversy here centers on circumcision as a necessity for salvation.

The Controversy Is Stated (15:1-5)

Christianity provokes *sharp dispute and debate* (NIV) or *no small dissention and debate* (NRSV) (see Acts 19:40; 23:7, 10). Lively debates frequently erupt around and within the new movement (see 1 Timothy 6:4; 2 Timothy 2:23). As noted in an earlier section (Part 3), the Christian church has always had its share of dissent and discord. Paul and Barnabas are still identified as the key and representative leadership of the Gentile missionary push. The elders and apostles represent a sort of final court to decide matters of practice.

With the deftness of an artist, Luke shows both the widespread acceptance of the Gentile mission in Samaria and Phoenicia as well as the source of the controversy. Opposition comes from a small group. The success of the

Gentile mission is the result of God's work. Resistance is centered in the Jerusalem church among former Pharisees. The Pharisees do believe in the hope of resurrection. They also insist on circumcision in order to fulfill the entire Mosaic Law. Scene one ends with the confrontation between strict religionists with their demands and the successful Christian missionaries with their universal implications.

Elders Gather; Peter's Speech (15:6-11)

Though the Pharisaic minority makes the charges, the apostles (including Peter) and the elders take charge of the congregational meeting. Scene two begins with a sharp focus on the leadership of the Jerusalem church. Peter begins his argument as if the matter has long since been settled. From the earliest days the Gentile mission has been authorized by God. God does the choosing (see 1 Samuel 16:9; 1 Kings 8:16; Nehemiah 9:7). Peter interprets the incidents surrounding the conversion of Cornelius as a precedent-setting event, even though for his original audience there was considerable question (compare 10:1 to 11:18).

No reference is made to an individual's tradition, race, or origin. Instead God looks upon who the individual is and whether that individual is worthy. Note the graceful suggestion that the Holy Spirit is given to the Gentiles, and then *we* are mentioned (see 10:44-47). Purity refers to God's cleansing of the heart, not to observance of religious ritual. Here, then, an additional reason for the Gentile mission has been introduced. God bestowed purity of heart on everyone, including the Gentiles.

Peter raises the level of his argument by asking a telling question: Since the entire missionary undertaking is God's design, how can Christians defy God? The use of the image of the *yoke* reveals just how strongly the Gentile Christians feel about traditional religious rituals.

A Hellenistic perspective on the law revels a burden that cannot be fulfilled.

Description of Gentile Mission (15:12-21)

The statement could easily have been that the Gentiles will be saved as we are. In verse 11 the statement is reversed. Thus scene two closes on a note of grace.

Scene three opens with silence. Evidently the strength of the argument has been sufficient to quiet the disturbance. Paul and Barnabas recall signs and wonders, both of which represent God's hand in the mission. Peter's argument is corroborated. In both narratives the apostles demonstrate clearly the fact that God has been at work at each critical juncture of the movement's outreach. The events themselves are not listed, as they have already been presented in chapters 13 and 14.

James assumes the role of leadership in the congregation.

Simeon is the Aramaic form of Peter's name. James employs one of the basic elements of kerygmatic preaching: The mission to the Gentiles fulfills the Old Testament promise made in Amos 9:11-12 (see also Jeremiah 12:15; Isaiah 45:21).

Luke uses the Scripture to interpret the significance of Jesus, not the restoration of the Davidic kingdom or of the true Israel. The reference includes an allusion to the significant event of the Resurrection. Not only will God seek the Gentiles, the Gentiles will seek the Lord.

The conclusion of the speech underscores what already has become obvious. Do not interfere with what God is doing. What is suggested is a compromise. Since they are unwilling or unable to do away with the entire tradition, the conservatives are willing to ask for concessions.

Polluted by idols is a reference to flesh offered to heathen gods. *Sexual immorality* (NIV) implies *fornication* (NRSV), which refers to the sanctity of marriage and a strong sense of morality. *Blood* refers to pagan rituals in which the blood of animals is drunk.

If Gentile Christians can observe these relatively minor concessions, then the debate will cease. Note that circumcision is not mentioned. The authority of Moses is attached to these restrictions.

Representatives Sent to Antioch (15:22-29)

Scene four opens with the acceptance of James' moderate proposal. Both the Jerusalem church and the Antiochan congregation are given an appropriate prestige. The Antiochan congregation is honored and authority still rests primarily with the Jerusalem church. The letter intends its authority to include the whole of Syria and Cilicia, which as yet have not been mentioned in Acts (Paul mentions these areas in his letter to the Galatians: see 1:21).

The salutation follows an accepted format (see Acts 23:26; James 1:1). The letter itself begins with a subtle denial of authority to the troublemakers. The disturbers acted on their own (see 15:1). The apostles' authority stems in part from their hazardous lives.

Two authorities now combine: the Holy Spirit and the earthly counsel concur. The only restrictions are relatively easy to tolerate. The letter closes with another customary formula.

Victory for the Gentile Mission (15:30-35)

Scene five closes out the Jerusalem Conference. The final episode takes place in the Antiochan congregation, where the letter is read. A celebration breaks out at the great new of compromise. Circumcision is not mentioned. The decision is a clear victory for the entire Gentile mission.

Judas and Silas have the authority to exhort, since they are prophets (see 1 Corinthians 14:3). Having been under considerable stress, and anxious about its fate, the congregation is now strengthened and reinforced by the preaching.

The amount of time that elapses is not at all clear. It could be less than a year. Verse 34 raises questions. Verse 40 suggests that Silas stays in Antioch, but verse 33 indicates that he was sent away. What is Luke's purpose? Luke could have been primarily interested in making Paul and Silas acquainted.

The entire episode concludes with Paul and Barnabas working together in Antioch prior to their final separation. The teaching (see 5:42) prepares the congregation to continue on its own through freeing the missionaries to continue their work in other areas. Luke shows that the vitality of the Christian congregation does not depend solely on specific persons of extraordinary gifts and graces. God sustains the congregation through the work of nameless but faithful people.

The harmonious resolution of a raging debate brings to an end the internal resistance to the gospel's universal implications. We cannot lose sight of how significant the victory is in the life of the church. By the same token, the impulse to resist the pull of the Holy Spirit is not restricted to a single generation of Christians.

Second Missionary Journey Begins (15:36-41)

Verse 36 begins a new section of Acts. Prior to this point the central question was whether or not there should be a Gentile mission (see 9:32–12:25). For the balance of Acts the Gentile mission is assumed. Paul initiates the second missionary journey. Luke lifts Paul to a position of authority. Some scholars suggest that at least part of Luke's purpose in Acts is to establish the authority and position of Paul. Luke's portrayal of the apostle certainly differs from Paul's own reflection about himself in his letters.

The second missionary journey begins with the intention to visit existing Christian congregations.

John Mark had returned to Jerusalem (see 13:13). Luke is not concerned with the detail of how he appears now in Antioch. The identity of John Mark varies. In Colossians 4:10 he is the cousin of Barnabas. Philemon 24 lists him, but this may not be the same Barnabas. Second Timothy 4:11 assumes the same identity.

Paul contends that the work of the mission is of central importance.

The conflict and separation do not damage the missionaries' work. Instead, their work expands. Barnabas sails to his homeland (see Acts 4:36). He is never mentioned again in Acts; however, in 1 Corinthians 9:6 he is presumed to be alive.

Luke spends very little time examining the ruptured relationship between Paul and Barnabas. Paul's own account differs in both degree and principle. Luke's narrative places an individual at the center of the conflict. Paul's account places a principle (celebration of the meal) at the center. Luke seems to use the story of John Mark to show Paul on his own.

In contrast to the departure of Barnabas, which seems quite unannounced, Paul receives an official sendoff (see 14:26). Luke underlines the importance of Paul's missionary journey. Silas is a very important Jerusalemite (see Acts 15:22).

Syria and Cilicia have been mentioned in the Apostolic Decree (15:23). Luke emphasizes the fact that it was not merely a local ordinance. The insights of Peter and Paul have become normative; so also have the decisions of the Jerusalem Conference for all Christians.

§ § § § § § §

The Message of Acts 15

In this chapter Luke presents the dramatic decision of the Jerusalem Conference and the beginning of Paul's second missionary journey. The internal resistance that had haunted the Christian missions earlier has ended. Now the missionaries can address their full energies to the tasks of missionary outreach.

The Jerusalem Conference is a victory for the missionaries and other Christians who see the implications of Jesus' gospel message.

What can we learn from this chapter?

§ God gives insight to people.

§ Insistence on strict adherence to religious ritual places burdens on people rather than blessings.

§ The congregations of God are sustained by the Holy Spirit and often include anonymous persons.

§ Conversions are evidence of God's work.

§ What God intends, people cannot long resist or deny.

§ Moderation and compromise are acceptable ways of resolving conflict.

§ Differences of opinion do not have to cripple a mission; they can serve to expand the scope of mission.

§ Luke implies a necessary correlation between earthly and divine authority in the Christian enterprise.

§ § § § § § §

Acts 16–17

Introduction to These Chapters

The description of the second missionary journey actually begins with Acts 15:36, as we have seen. Chapters 16 and 17 continue narrating this journey. Readers should keep in mind Luke's purpose for using the material. Recall that specific instances represent wider events as well as individual circumstances. As the Christian mission continues, the gospel makes its advance both territorially and culturally. Luke shows much greater interest in the latter two journey than he does the first.

Here is an outline of 16:1–17:15:
  I. Derbe and Lystra (16:1-5)
 II. Phrygia, Galatia, and Troas (16:6-10)
III. In Philippi (16:11-15)
 IV. Conflict and Arrest (16:16-24)
  V. Imprisonment and Vindication (16:25-40)
 VI. To Thessalonica (17:1-9)
VII. A Narrow Escape (17:10-15)

Derbe and Lystra (16:1-5)

The journey begins with passage through the regions of Syria and Cilicia. In Lystra, Paul meets with the young disciple who had been converted during the earlier journey (see 1 Corinthians 4:17). Even though a hard battle had been fought in the Jerusalem Conference regarding circumcision, Paul circumcises the young man.

Had Paul disregarded the decision? Does Luke imply a disregard for the hard-won victory? Perhaps Luke uses this particular narrative to illustrate Paul's intense desire not to offend Jews. Paul asserts that he become like a Jew to win Jews (see 1 Corinthians 9:20), and the same might hold true for Timothy as well.

Luke concludes this section by the statement that growth in the congregations indicates divine blessing.

Phrygia, Galatia, and Troas (16:6-10)

Paul had begun the journey with the express intention of revisiting established congregations (see Acts 15:36). Soon, however, the intervention of the Holy Spirit changes the itinerary. This is not primarily Paul's design. Luke indicates that at every significant turning point the Holy Spirit directs or influences the events. The narrative reminds us of the Cornelius episode, in which a completely new direction is taken. In this instance an entirely new region is opened up to the Christian movement by divine intervention and leading. Luke does suggest that the human element is also present. After all, the missionaries must comprehend and decide to heed the direction.

Mysia is the territory in the northwestern region of present-day Turkey. Troas is on the coast of the Aegean Sea. The region of Macedonia is a Roman province in southeastern Europe. It includes Philippi, Thessalonica, and Beroea.

In verse 10 the *we* passages begin. Following the vision of the Macedonian, Luke employs the literary technique of the eyewitness account. The identity of the writer is difficult to ascertain. It certainly is not Paul. It may well be Silas or Timothy, since both of these men are described in close relationship with the journey (see 16:3-5). In any event, the use of the pronoun serves to include the readers in the dramatic narratives and to allow us to feel the fortunes of the missionaries as our own.

In Philippi (16:11-15)

Traveling a direct course through Neapolis (present-day Cavalle), a port second in importance only to Thessalonica, the missionaries reach the harbor city of Philippi. The city was originally settled by supporters of Anthony from Italy. Macedonia had been divided into four administrative areas in order to prevent widespread revolt.

The missionaries begin their work in the place of prayer on a sabbath day. Perhaps the missionaries have to work at least part of the time for their own living. If that is the case, they might have only a single day each week that they could use as free time to preach.

Lydia sells goods that are obviously a luxury for the wealthy. Almost immediately the narrative shifts to her baptism, which marks her clearly as a Christian. Luke uses this brief narrative to show that Christianity has now secured a congregation in the city.

Conflict and Arrest (16:16-24)

Were the missionaries returning to the same location? This scene suggests a similar movement as in 16:13. Christianity again confronts heathen belief, in this instance a young girl exploited for her peculiar gifts. From her mouth comes a description of Christian preachers that Gentiles can understand. Luke uses the incident not only as a miracle of exorcism but also to illustrate how even pagans could recognize the meaning of the Christian mission.

The *we* passages not cease until their recurrence in Acts 20:5.

Silas and Paul are dragged into the public market place and accosted by an anti-Semitic crowd. The charges have nothing to do with exorcism; it is not a punishable offense. The missionaries have disturbed the peace. By confronting the exploitation of a woman and freeing her from abuse, Christians disrupted the status quo. What better charge for any Christian than disturbing the false peace of a status quo? Whipping follows (see 2 Corinthians 11:25; 1 Thessalonians 2:2).

Imprisonment and Vindication (16:25-40)

Luke uses vivid descriptions in order to emphasize the terrible loneliness and suffering endured by Silas and Paul. Unlike the silence of Peter during his imprisonment, Silas and Paul pray and sing. Incredibly, the foundations shake (see Acts 4:31) and the chains fall away. Through pitch darkness Paul prevents a suicide. Only then does the stunned jailer call for torches.

Terrified and thoroughly shaken, the jailer asks the basic question about salvation. The apostles' response assures the jailer, his entire family, and the servants (see 11:14).

Apparently unconcerned about what the higher authorities will do about the escaped prisoners, the jailer tends to the missionaries' wounds. After that, he himself is baptized. Perhaps through this story Luke intends to show the power of a higher authority.

Saner heads prevail during the night hours. The disciples are to be released. Therefore the jailer is saved from punishment. But Paul adamantly refuses a quiet dismissal. Public vindication must follow public humiliation. Paul has identified the authorities' breaking of the law. Paul achieves the public statement, but is evicted anyway.

As the missionaries leave, Luke leaves the reader with the knowledge that yet another Christian congregation has been established. Moreover, Luke has employed the various aspects of the narrative to illustrate the remarkable power of Christianity. The Holy Spirit directs the journey, arranges for the exorcism, performs a miraculous release, and finally uses peculiar circumstances to establish a Christian presence. Paul, of course, is seen in a bright light. This narrative serves the purpose of recovering Paul's importance in the Christian missionary enterprise.

To Thessalonica (17:1-9)

No activity seems to occur in either Amphipolis or Apollonia. These cities are simply points on a journey. The synagogue, still important to the missionary work, is located in Thessalonica. Thessalonica is the capital city of the second district of the Roman province of Macedonia. The proconsul lives in this city.

Three sabbath days means three consecutive sabbaths, not necessarily a period of three weeks. Paul speaks here in the context of worship. (See also Acts 17:17; 18:4; 19:8.) He uses the Old Testament Scriptures as his evidence. His preaching centers on the suffering Messiah (see 3:18; Luke 24:26, 46). This was a notion absolutely repugnant to Jewish listeners. Paul then proclaims Jesus as the Messiah.

Upperclass women along with others are drawn to the faith. But these women will not be able to prevent persecution. Christian success threatens Jewish gains, and a riot erupts.

Jason is a Greek name that is similar to the Hebrew Joshua, or Jesus. Jason did receive the missionaries and is therefore accused of collaboration against the Roman Caesar (see John 19:12; 1 Peter 2:17). Bail is posted and the men are released. Note that this brief narrative has no reference to the intervention of the Holy Spirit.

A Narrow Escape (17:10-15)

Without any delay Luke places the missionaries in Beroea, some twenty-two miles from Thessalonica. Again, the missionaries begin their work in a synagogue.

The Jews in this city are described as men of piety. A

Christian congregation begins (20:4 assumes a Christian congregation in Beroea), not only with common folk, but with higher class people as well.

Word of God means the missionary preaching. Luke makes no effort to explain how the Thessalonians are able to stir up the riot. Paul is dispatched immediately to sea. But Silas remains in the city with Timothy, who appears without any explanation (we last saw him in Acts 16:3). Luke is quite unconcerned about secondary characters and explanations of their movement. In 1 Thessalonians 3:1-2, Timothy is supposed to have accompanied Paul to Athens. Even though Silas and Timothy remain in Beroea, they later meet Paul in Corinth (see 18:1-5).

Before going on to the consideration of the next major setting of Paul's work, we would be wise to examine the way Luke uses Paul's missionary work. From chapter 13 on, Paul's work always results in the formation of another Christian congregation. Central in Paul's work is his preaching of the suffering Messiah who is raised from the dead. Resurrection is always a significant element in the kerygma. When the Christian missionary effort successfully attracts people to faith, persecution inevitably follows. Occasionally Luke describes the preaching more fully (see 13:15-41) or combines a miracle with the successful Christian congregation (see 14:8-10). In all instances the Holy Spirit uses the opportunities of reception and resistance to establish or spread the Christian gospel.

§ § § § § § §

The Message of Acts 16–17

Luke's account of Paul's second missionary journey takes the reader across Asia Minor (through Syria and Cilicia) toward the Asian continent. The Holy Spirit presses the missionaries toward Europe instead. Through careful use of these events, Luke draws attention not only to Paul but also to the continued work of the Holy Spirit through Paul.

Especially significant is the interpretation of the direct intervention of the Holy Spirit when the missionaries intended to revisit established churches. On the surface it must have looked to the frustrated missionaries like a failure of their mission. They could not go where they had planned to go.

As a result, the missionaries had to make adjustments and take their work in a completely different direction. We might even say that they had to take a challenging course through the unknown rather than the comfortable path of revisiting well-known territory and familiar people. Along this line, the Gospel of John concludes with the poignant scene in which Jesus speaks of the time when the disciples (and the church) will have to go where they don't want to go (see John 21:18-19).

What else can we learn from our examination of these two chapters in Acts?

§ Paul could make adjustments in his behavior without sacrificing his principles.

§ Paul preached to whoever came to hear him. We see that he trusted in his message rather than the numbers of people who listened.

§ The gospel of Christ appeals to all classes of society: the high (wealthy women), the low (the servant girl), and the workers (the Philippian jailer).

§ Even in the most lonely circumstances, God remains with the faithful.

§ God can use what appears to be failure to fulfill the divine purpose.

§ The suffering Messiah is authenticated by faithful persons willing to suffer on his behalf.

§ § § § § § §

Introduction to This Chapter

We concluded the previous part with Paul's hasty
departure from the unrest in Beroea. Timothy and Silas
remained behind in order to strengthen the congregation;
they will meet Paul later. Luke now focuses solely on
Paul's work in new and challenging mission fields. The
issues which had spawned internal resistance have been
resolved. The resolution came at a good time, since now
the Christian movement begins to evoke more
antagonism from a variety of sources. It will need all the
internal strength it can muster.

Here is an outline of Acts 17:16–18:22:
    I. Paul in Athens (17:16-21)
   II. Paul's Speech in the Areopagus (17:22-31)
  III. Responses to Paul's Speech (17:32-34)
  IV. Paul in Corinth (18:1-4)
   V. Timothy and Silas Arrive (18:5-11)
  VI. More Resistance (18:12-17)
 VII. To Syria and Antioch (18:18-22)

Paul in Athens (17:16-21)

Athens was a relatively small city at the time when
Acts was written, with 5,000 citizens. With the
introductory words in verse 16, Luke prepares the reader
for verses 22 and following. Verse 16 shows Paul very
disturbed by idols which clearly are not works of art.

In their earlier work the missionaries preached

primarily in Jewish synagogues and on the sabbath. Paul, however, preaches to whoever will listen in the marketplace. At least part of the genius of the Christian movement in the apostolic period and in other eras of change is that Christian preachers sought people where they were. Often people were found in marketplaces, in streets, and in fields.

Epicureans are materialistic and very practical. To them Paul is little more than a babbler. Here the term *babbler* is a play on the Greek word meaning cock-sparrow, a bird that picks up scraps. Paul merely picks up random ideas, according to these philosophers who are criticizing him.

Stoics represent other people in Athens who are not antagonistic to the Christian message.

Paul is either brought before the authorities (the Council of the Areopagus) or taken to Mars Hill, away from the frenetic marketplace. The tone of the question in verse 19 suggests interest, but certainly not antagonism.

Luke characterizes the Athenians as always curious and looking for the next new idea that might stimulate their curiosity and thinking.

Paul's Speech in the Areopagus (17:22-31)

Paul now assumes the role of orator (see also Acts 2:14; 5:20; 27:21). He begins with a benevolent description of the Athenians. Evidently the request for clarification (see verse 20) plus the inscription mentioned in verse 23 moves Paul to end their ignorance by interpreting his Christian perspective. The argumentative, sometimes almost antagonistic tone of Paul's other preaching is absent in this sermon.

Paul begins with Scripture. He uses words similar to those in Isaiah 42:5, which summarize the Creation narratives (see Genesis 1:1-23). Citing both the Law and the Prophets, Paul declares the biblical God to be both Creator and Lord of heaven and earth. This God cannot be found in buildings or idols. Neither will this God receive sacrifices (see 7:42-43).

Again Paul cites the Creation narratives to emphasize the true intention of God and God's creation.

God intends for human beings to have two responsibilities: to make themselves at home on earth in their appropriate places and to seek God. This same God of Creation is still near to everyone.

Paul quotes from Greek poets, citing Epimenides and Aratus' *Phaenomena* (see Colossians 1:17; Hebrews 1:3).

Having established God as the name for which Greeks had searched, Paul now addresses the specific issue of pagan idol or image worship. Here he draws on the Hebrew biblical traditions that attack idol worship (see, for example, Deuteronomy 4:28; Isaiah 40:18-19; 44:9-20; Acts 19:26).

The sermon up to this point has concentrated solely on God as Creator and Lord. Now Paul introduces the notion of repentance. Through preaching, ignorance is eliminated. This repentance is required since a day of judgment fast approaches with the threat of retribution (see Psalms 9:5; 96:13; 97:1-5).

By a man clearly refers to Jesus. The Resurrection is offered as proof of the entire claim.

Responses to Paul's Speech (17:32-34)

Since the listeners are not Jewish and probably are unfamiliar with the notion of resurrection, they have two different reactions. Some of the listeners scoff at such preposterous nonsense. Others will wait to hear more.

Remember that the scene began with Paul summarily escorted to defend himself. Following his sermon he successfully removes himself from a potentially violent confrontation. Even though this sermon is, because of the circumstances, a different kind of preaching, Christian converts still join the movement (see 14:15-17). However, no baptism is mentioned.

Luke's purpose in this incident is to show Christianity's encounter with the entire Greek world. For the Greeks, too, the doctrine of resurrection is a very real stumbling block (1 Corinthians 1:23).

Paul in Corinth (18:1-4)

Corinth is the capital city in the Roman province of Achaia. Its frontage on two seas made it an excellent commercial city. Along with its reputation as a trade center, it had the Temple of Aphrodite and 1,000 prostitutes. Thus, Corinth was also notorious due to its flagrant immorality.

Aquila is a Jew displaced by Claudius' decree of banishment. Aquila and Priscilla probably have a house church, though clearly Luke does not mean to imply that these two people began the mission.

A tentmaker would have been a leather worker, not a weaver. Paul has had to make a living as well as spend his time preaching.

Since Luke uses *the*, he implies that there is only one synagogue in the entire city. (See verse 7 also.)

Timothy and Silas Arrive (18:5-11)

The arrival of Silas and Timothy (recall Acts 17:15) with a gift allows Paul to preach full time. Throughout all the Christian enterprise thus far, preaching addressed mainly Jews. Now Paul reaches the limits of his own tolerances. No longer will he preach to Jews, since they refuse to heed Christian salvation (see Acts 13:46; 28:28).

In Paul's estimation he can now continue preaching to Gentiles. In one sense this decision frees Paul to pursue his preaching mission energetically and without worry about the response to his words by the Jews.

However, in another sense, this is a real tragedy. Jewish people exclude themselves from the Christian hope. The tragedy has been deepened throughout history by Christians who condemn any who exclude themselves. Extreme care and caution need to characterize our use of this text and others like it.

Some scholars identify Titius Justus as Titus. Crispus is one of the few people Paul baptized (see 1 Corinthians 1:14). As leader of the synagogue, his conversion would impress others and lead the way for further conversions.

A vision of Christ during the night confirms not only the ongoing presence of Christ, but the presence of other faithful Christians as well. The image is reminiscent of God's encouragement for Elijah as he confronted the challenge of witnessing in a hostile region (see 1 Kings 19:18). The image also recalls God's promise in Isaiah 43:5.

More Resistance (18:12-17)

Gallio (Marcus Annaeus Novatus) is the brother of Seneca, the philosopher. He was proconsul in Asia in about A.D. 51. Gallio's attitude is anti-Semitic, and he is convinced that the difficulty is little more than arguments over words (see 26:3).

Verses 14-16 make the point that Christianity is not a violent movement. At least part of Luke's purpose in the book of Acts is to show Christianity poses no threat to Roman authority and order.

To Syria and Antioch (18:18-22)

After a year and a half (verse 11), Paul departs along with Priscilla (who is always named first; see also verse 26; Romans 16:3; 2 Timothy 4:19). Luke makes no attempt to explain Paul's ritual of haircutting at Cenchreae. Perhaps, like the instance of Timothy's circumcision (see 16:3), Luke hints at Paul's Jewish heritage.

Ephesus is the capital city and residence of the proconsul of the Roman province of Asia, and a commercial center. The two business owners are left behind, perhaps to give reason for Paul's return at a later time. The second missionary journey ends somewhat abruptly as Paul returns to Antioch.

§ § § § § § §

The Message of Acts 18

The second missionary journey focuses primarily on Paul. Even though the Gentile mission has been approved, Paul still continues preaching to Jewish audiences in synagogues. Only after Jews refuse the Christian message does Paul turn primarily to Gentiles. We see that Paul very reluctantly turns away from the Jewish tradition. Indeed, twice during the journey he complies with ancient customs. The triumph of Christianity is accompanied by the tragedy of those who exclude themselves from the gospel.

What can we learn from these chapters?

§ God is the God of all Creation.

§ In a world where people like to banter about ideas, the truth of Christ needs to be proclaimed. God assures Christians of continued support both by the Holy Spirit and through other faithful people.

§ Even though we may not know who they are, other people hold fast to the faith.

§ God does not have to be searched for; God is present with all persons.

§ Christianity is not a violent movement.

§ Christians do not turn their backs on people—other people turn their backs on Christianity.

§ § § § § § §

Second Missionary Journey

Antioch (15:36-40)

Syria and Cilicia (15:41)
  Derbe (16:1)
  Lystra (16:1-5)
  Iconium (16:1-5)

Phrygia and Galatia (16:6-7)
  Troas (16:8-9)

Philippi (16:10-40)

Thessalonica (17:1-9)

Beroea (17:10-14)

Athens (17:15-34)

Corinth (18:1-17)

Ephesus (18:18-21)

Caesarea (18:22)

Antioch (18:22-23)

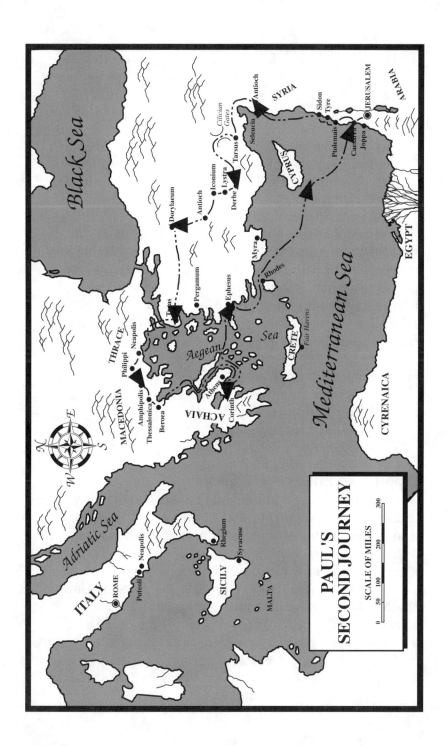

PAUL'S
SECOND JOURNEY

SCALE OF MILES

0   50 100   200   300

Acts 19

Introduction to This Chapter

The NRSV begins the third journey of Paul in the middle of chapter 18, at verse 23. Therefore, we begin this section of the commentary at that point. Luke very quickly summarizes the final portion of Paul's second journey, without giving any information about his 1,400-mile travels. Luke seems anxious to get on to the final missionary journey.

Here is an outline of chapters 18:23–19:41:
 I. Apollos in Ephesus (18:23-28)
 II. Paul in Ephesus (19:1-20)
 III. Paul Plans for the Journey to Rome (19:21-22)
 IV. A Riot Started by Demetrius (19:23-41)

Apollos in Ephesus (18:23-28)

An indefinite amount of time passes between the second and third journeys. Like the second journey, this one begins with visiting existing congregations. Luke summarizes the events by saying all the disciples are strengthened. Perhaps the disciples include not only those in the congregations, but also the missionaries themselves. Surely their own spirits would be encouraged by the faithful witness of scores of anonymous Christians.

Apollos is a native of Alexandria, and therefore would interpret Scripture allegorically. He is well educated about both the Hebrew Scriptures and the traditions of Jesus. However, he teaches only the baptism of John (the Baptist).

Unaware of the limits of his message, Apollos challenges the congregation in the synagogue with his preaching. Since Luke says that Apollos knew only the baptism of John, we can anticipate Priscilla and Aquila correcting him, especially in this and the baptist of the Holy Spirit.

A Christian congregation exists in Ephesus. It offers support to the intentions of Apollos. When he arrives in Ephesus, not only is he helped but he further strengthens the Christian congregation. Evidently his argument and preaching are sufficiently powerful to warrant a new mission field.

This short episode provides a direct link with Paul in the next chapter.

Paul in Ephesus (19:1-20)

Paul's two-year ministry in Ephesus (see verse 10); compare 20:31) provides not only rich material but the background for 1 and 2 Corinthians.

Paul travels the region of Galatia in Asia Minor (see 18:23). Upon arriving in Ephesus Paul meets Christian disciples. Following his earlier decision, and in contrast to earlier missions, he does not enter the synagogue at first.

For some undisclosed reason, Paul has doubts about these Christians with respect to the Holy Spirit. Further clarification reveals only the baptism characterized by repentance, without reference to the name of Jesus.

John the Baptist preached that people should look for another to follow him. After the Baptist's death a movement developed around his teachings. Clearly Paul has encountered one of those sects. After Paul's clarification the disciples are baptized in the name of Jesus (see 8:14-17). This should not be constructed as a second baptism or rebaptism. Some scholars suggest that Aquila performs the baptism.

With the laying on of hands the promised Holy Spirit comes and the disciples begin ecstatic (pneumatic) utterances and prophecies. Paul differentiates the tongues from regular language (see 1 Corinthians 14:4-5).

The scene closes with twelve disciples fully informed about the Christian way. Luke has subtly kept Paul in the forefront since his companions corrected Apollos (18:24-48), and here Paul corrects the Baptist's disciples.

Paul, in Ephesus, continues his missionary work. This long ministry is the highest point of his work, and the last time he pursues his work freely.

Acts 18:19 had prepared the way for Paul's appearance in the synagogue. Paul debates regularly in a lecture hall. Tyrannus (verse 9) may have been a teacher or schoolmaster.

With a single sentence (verse 10), Luke states in broad strokes Paul's incredible achievement and authority. During this two-year time period all of Asia hears the Christian gospel: the Mysians, the Lydians, the Carians. New congregations are established in Colossai and Laodicea.

Luke further emphasizes Paul's authority through miracle stories. Recall that Paul had already performed an exorcism in Corinth, thus proving his apostolic authority. The miracles are accomplished through what Paul touches (recall the healing shadow in 5:12-15). Scholars point out that this miraculous and public power seems to contradict Paul's own witness that Christ's strength is shown in weakness (see 2 Corinthians 12:9). The church holds Paul in highest esteem. This is due in no small measure to the work of Luke in writing Acts. There will always be a tension between the demand of the cross and the joy of triumph and glory; one does not negate the other. They must be kept in tension and balance. The potential for evil comes when one of the two truths is deleted altogether.

Exorcisms are not limited to Paul (see 16:16-18; Mark 9:38; Matthew 12:27). Here the magician has no personal relationship with the power. He has picked up the name of Jesus without the internal changes necessary to use it. Jesus' name is not magic. Since the magicians have no real power, they are overwhelmed by the man and flee, naked.

Luke concludes this section with the feelings of wonder and awe so frequently mentioned in Acts (see 2:43; 3:10; 4:13; 9:35; 13:12; 15:12; 16:34).

In this brief episode (verses 11-20) Luke accomplishes three objectives. First, he shows that no one can imitate Paul, thus emphasizing Paul's authority. Second, he shows Christianity's break from magic. In a more general sense, however, he points out the liability of secondhand faith when confronting any authentic human problem. Christians must have a person relationship with God if they expect to witness in Jesus' name in a world that will not readily or easily concede authority to any name.

Ephesus was known for its magic. The books mentioned in verse 19 would have been either parchment or papyrus leaves, and obviously expensive. A public book burning illustrates the magnitude of the charges brought by Christianity. The Christian movement prospers and the word of God prevails.

Paul Plans for the Journey to Rome (19:21-22)

Luke characterizes Paul's plans in an ambiguous way. *In the Spirit* implies the leading of the Holy Spirit. (The NIV does not use the phrase but translates as *Paul decided*.) But there is also room for Paul's own responsibility for making plans after prayers and the presence of the Spirit with him. No reason for the journey is given. Perhaps the journey was for the collection to which he refers in his letters (see also Acts

24:17). Paul's journey turns out to be a frustrating visit to Corinth, and then through Macedonia to Jerusalem (see 2 Corinthians 2:12-13; Acts 20:1-3).

Timothy appears again in a relatively minor role. In Paul's letters he is given much larger standing (see Romans 16:21; 1 Corinthians 4:17; 2 Corinthians 1:1; Philippians 1:1; also the pastoral letters). Titus, along with other unnamed Christians, resolved the Corinthian crisis (see 2 Corinthians 12:18). Erastus is mentioned in Romans 16:23 and 2 Timothy 4:20).

A Riot Started by Demetrius (19:23-41)

Demetrius instigates a riot in Ephesus. The situation in Ephesus has become increasingly volatile. Christianity has made a remarkable impact and now poses a threat to certain economic and religious interests. Artemis is the city's major divinity. The Temple of Artemis was one of the seven wonders of the ancient world. Demetrius is the guildmaster or chief of a very important industry.

Paul's reputation as well as the results of his preaching are well known (recall the speech in the Aeropagus, 17:29-34). Religion aside, the sheer economic disruption is sufficient to stir vehement unrest. The mob erupts into mass confusion.

The Ephesus theater held as many as 24,000 people. Aristarchus is mentioned elsewhere by Paul (see Colossians 4:10; Philemon 24). Gaius is from Derbe (see Romans 16:23; 3 John 1).

Luke suggests no motive for Paul's desire to go to the theater. Perhaps it is his conscience or reliance on his Roman citizenship. In any event, disciples prevent his going.

Asiarchs (verse 31) serve the political function of securing loyalty to Rome. In their care they advise Paul not to enter the fray. Luke once again uses a subtle detail to show how Roman authority does not have to fear the Christian movement. The scene is one of total chaos and gross ignorance. The anti-Semitic mob cannot tell the difference between a Jew and a Christian. Clearly Jews feel threatened. As Alexander, a Jew, attempts to make a defense, the mob in turn shouts him down with the catch phrase already stated by Demetrius.

The town clerk's responsibility is to carry out the wishes of the popular assembly. At long last he gains control of the riot. Cities and individuals were occasionally awarded the title *keeper of the god*. He appeals to their civic and religious pride. Ephesus is well known for Artemis; therefore Demetrius' volatile charge has no real basis. Gaius and Aristarchus are neither vandals nor blasphemers.

In any event, if charges are to be brought there are official legal procedures through which the rabble-rousing Demetrius can pursue his case. The argument carries the hour and the mob disperses.

Luke presents a vivid incident in which the local economy and religion have been threatened by Christianity. Interestingly, not the first word of Christian preaching is mentioned. Neither Paul nor any of the disciples preach. What is clear is the impact of preaching in other areas and cities. Christian preaching in Ephesus may cause similar disruptions. Previously Christian conscience refused to allow the slave girl to be exploited. Now the Christian conscience disrupts idolatry and an economy dependent upon religious trinkets. Luke's account of Demetrius' fear, the craftsmen's anxiety, and the subsequent riot shows, as if by its shadow, the enormous power of the Christian message, especially through Paul.

§ § § § § § §

The Message of Acts 19

The Christian movement encounters many challenges. Through graphic vignettes Luke tells his readers how the earliest Christians met these challenges. Clearly, he intends to instruct his readers on how they too can effectively give witness when confronted by antagonists or questions.

What can we learn from these verses?

§ Not only does the major preacher have responsibility to preach; all Christians have a responsibility to witness.

§ God uses helpers as well as major, central figures.

§ Christians are aware of the Holy Spirit and are able to receive the Holy Spirit.

§ Christian preaching poses a real challenge to anyone who exploits others.

§ Antagonists of Christianity can only shout themselves hoarse when confronted by the truth of God.

§ Actions substantiate Christian claims of power.

§ Religion cannot be used in a secondhand way with any great effect.

§ Christianity has nothing to do with magic.

§ When Christianity begins to address the economy, vested interests will feel threatened and want to fight.

§ § § § § § §

Acts 20

Introduction to This Chapter

In this chapter we will follow Paul through the end of his final missionary journey. (The description of Paul's third journey ends at 21:16.) Luke continues to lift Paul to the heights of authority and power through preaching. Luke's other themes are still emphasized. Christianity still advances in the face of increasingly violent opposition. The riot in Ephesus could not stop Christianity's impact. Increasingly, Paul's work aims toward Jerusalem and eventually Rome itself.

Here is an outline of Acts 20:1–21:16:
I. Paul Travels On (20:1-6)
II. The Raising of Eutychus (20:7-12)
III. Toward Palestine (20:13-38)
IV. More Ports of Call (21:1-6)

Paul Travels On (20:1-6)

Paul does not have to flee from Ephesus. Some scholars suggest that Paul may have stayed for many months. Luke says Paul *encourages* the disciples before he leaves. Encourage may include comforting and other elements of kerygmatic preaching. Here we see evidence that preaching is to be of vital significance to Luke as well as the church in the apostolic era.

Macedonia includes the cities of Philippi, Thessalonica, and Beroea, with which Paul has worked. Romans

15:22-29 suggests that Paul wrote to the Romans at this same time.

Another plot forces Paul to alter his plans. The journey must be completed since Paul and his companions are carrying relief money to Jerusalem (see Acts 24:17; 1 Corinthians 16:1-4; 2 Corinthians 8:20).

Luke lists seven companions: Sopater of Beroea, son of Pyrrhus (possibly the *Sosipater* mentioned in Romans 16:21); two men from Thessalonica, Aristarchus and Secundus (19:29; 27:2); Gaius of Derbe; Timothy, with whom readers are familiar and therefore he receives no further explanation; and two Asians, Tychicus and Trophimus (see 21:29; Ephesians 6:21). The narrator also includes himself in this entourage.

The group left Philippi *after the days* (NRSV) or *feast* (NIV) of *Unleavened Bread*. This annual feast commemorated the Exodus from Egypt, and was celebrated in conjunction with Passover.

Raising of Eutychus (10:7-12)

The first day of the week (verse 7) is Sunday. Here this identification is made for the first time.

Luke assumes that there is a Christian congregation in Troas. As with many congregations throughout the earlier chapters of Acts, Luke makes no attempt to explain how the congregation was established. Paul could have been responsible. (See Acts 20:1-6; 2 Corinthians 2:12-13.)

Luke details the setting. The vapors from the lights cause Eutychus to fall asleep. The accident is not the result of darkness. Perhaps the detail is included in order to correct the suspicion that Christians gather in clandestine groups under cover of darkness.

Paul's action is strongly reminiscent of the Hebrew Scripture's tradition of Elijah (1 Kings 17:21-24) and Elisha (2 Kings 4:32-37). Note that Paul does not say his soul is still in him.

The entire congregation celebrates the communion and

continues worship until daybreak. Luke concludes the episode, emphasizing the boy's life.

The story roughly parallels the narrative of Peter and Tabitha (see Acts 9:36-43). In both cases a young person is raised from death. In Paul's episode the miraculous power of the apostle underscores his authority, especially as he continues his missionary journey.

Toward Palestine (20:13-38)

Initially the companions prepare for a journey by sea. Paul, however, takes a shorter overland route. Luke gives no reason for Paul's decision; perhaps he wants to avoid the dangerous voyage. He could very possibly have wanted to be alone with God.

Mitylene is the capital city of Lesbos, about forty-four miles from Assos. Miletus, modern-day Parlat, is at the mouth of the river Maeander.

Paul avoids Ephesus on the return journey. Presumably the vessel does not dock there. As we have seen repeatedly, Luke is not concerned with the explanation of details in these narratives. Instead, his emphasis is on Paul, once a very pious Jew, desiring to be in Jerusalem for the celebration of Pentecost.

Even though the Christian movement expands with surprising speed, the traditions of Judaism from which it emerged still have a claim on Paul. We have seen Paul observe tradition through both circumcision of Timothy and through cutting his hair.

Luke's purpose of retaining and respecting the roots from which Christianity grows shows very clearly. At least one aspect of maturity is not having to curse or deny our origins and past or be cursed by them. The immature generally want to deny what they have been out of embarrassment or fear of feeling cursed by what is in the past (and cannot be retrieved or redone).

Christians run a great risk when they attempt to deny their origins in Judaism. Luke's presentation of Paul's pious intention suggests to all Christians *not* to reject all of Jewish tradition and culture.

Paul's farewell differs from other speeches he has made. To begin with, he addresses the elders of the church, that is, the clergy. This is the only speech in all of Acts addressed primarily to clergy. The speech also hints at difficulties confronting the churches Paul established in Asia.

Paul begins the first section with a backward glance to Ephesus. The elders are the first who were converted by Paul's missionary work. Paul characterizes life, and life of the clergy generally, by humility (verse 19), tears (verse 31), and persecution (verses 22-23). The description is not only of what was but also of what will be.

The true apostolic faith and proclamation must be held in utmost importance. Perhaps Luke is alluding to a time when the faith would be attacked, or lost to heresy.

Apostolic preaching is condensed and summarized in repentance and faith in the Lord Jesus Christ.

Present circumstances form the second section. In all the journeys the Holy Spirit directs the work and compels Paul to do the Spirit's intention. In response, he can do nothing else. The duty of an apostle is all Paul wants to accomplish (see 2 Timothy 4:7; Philippians 3:14).

However, Paul's confession has a certain mystery about it. He speaks about completing the course. Does this imply martyrdom at the end of this life? Clearly, Paul understand two truths about the Christian life. First, the Holy Spirit has first claim on the Christian's life and energies. We can only wonder how many times Paul may have wanted to do otherwise than the Spirit indicated.

We don't like to hear mundane words about duty and responsibility. We prefer words like achievement and authority. But Paul's witness and Luke's reaffirmation state clearly that Christian virtue frequently takes the form of humble obedience.

Paul manages to heed the Spirit's intention, whatever the cost. This brings us to the second truth, that the Christian life may well be one literally expended on behalf of the gospel.

Future concerns form the third section of the address. The Ephesians and all congregations will not see Paul again. But since he has fulfilled his responsibility of preaching and leading, should congregations stray from the faith, he is not to be blamed.

The whole will (NIV) or *purpose of God* (NRSV) (verse 27) implies the integrity and faithfulness of the Christian proclamation. Previously, in Ephesus, we heard about the Christian preaching only through the explanation of an opponent (Demetrius). Here Paul seems to be suggesting a possible heresy beginning in the church. Otherwise he would not have to characterize his own preaching as the whole counsel of God.

The shepherd image is very important in ministry (see Jeremiah 23:2; Zechariah 11:16; John 10:11 and 21:5-17).

Heresy will affect the church from both within and without. The heresy to which Luke alludes through Paul's speech is the Gnostic heresy which swept through many churches during the first and second centuries. The Gnostics believed, among other things, that true knowledge of God is available only to a chosen few. Their name drives from the Greek word *gnosis*, which means *knowledge*.

The fourth and final section is a blessing and a reminder of Christian care. Ministers are not to exploit their congregations, nor is wealth to be coveted.

The words of Jesus that Paul cites are not found in any of the four Gospels.

The final scene is one of poignant simplicity. The apostle kneels with his people to pray. Departure evokes immense grief and the entire congregation weeps. Prayer both concludes the relationship and initiates the last leg of the return journey. These Christians will never see Paul again (see verse 25).

More Ports of Call (21:1-16)

On the return leg of the second journey, Luke shows little concern for the details of episodes or incidents. In this return, however, a little more detail of the trip is given. Paul travels from Miletus to Cos, to Rhodes, and then to Patara, with no separations in between.

Tyre has a congregation, but no mention is made of its founding. These unknown Christians perceive through the Holy Spirit that Paul should not proceed to Jerusalem. But Paul has already intimated that he understands his end (see Acts 20:23). Congregational support fortifies Paul for the inevitable stress.

Ptolemais is near Haifa. Again an anonymous Christian congregation greets the traveler. Caesarea is about forty miles from Ptolemais and would have been a long journey for one day. Caesarea is the home of Philip, so the congregations there may have been founded by one of the original Seven (see 6:5; also 8:40).

The four daughters illustrate the detailed itinerary, but reveal nothing else about Paul or what awaits him in Jerusalem. Recall that Luke's Gospel emphasizes Jesus' intention of going to Jerusalem (see Luke 9:51-56). In Acts, too, Paul must go to Jerusalem, following not only the example of Jesus but the command of the Holy Spirit.

Agabus (recall 11:28) reappears. Caesarea is also in the administrative district of Judea.

The girdle is a long cloth garment wound several times around the body, in which money would often be kept (see Matthew 10:9). This should not be interpreted as an indication of impending martyrdom (see John 21:18-19). The symbolic act reminds Luke's readers of Hebrew prophets' symbolic acts (see Isaiah 20:2-6; Jeremiah 13:1-9).

The incident draws attention to the strong parallel between Jesus and Paul. Both are delivered into the hands of the authorities. Accusations prevent release, and Paul is not ignorant of his future (see Romans 15:30-33). He certainly does not proceed blindly.

The will of God is uppermost in Paul's (and Luke's) mind (see Luke 22:42). Even Paul's closest companions must concede to the inevitable. Paul returns to Jerusalem.

§ § § § § § §

The Message of Acts 20

During the final leg of the third journey the story gathers momentum. Paul becomes increasingly anxious to return to Jerusalem. The regions into which he has journeyed exhibit resilient, if obscure, Christian congregations. In large measure, Paul's work has been remarkably successful. Like his Lord, Paul must complete the will of God, which he does in the face of all sorts of resistance, both hostile and friendly.

What can we learn from these chapters?

§ Christian gatherings more often than not include preaching; preaching strengthens the Christian community.

§ Mature Christians must know what their duty is and have sufficient will to do it.

§ Resistance to duty can be either hostile or friendly.

§ Christians need time alone with God for adequate preparation for difficult tasks.

§ The faith will sometimes be threatened by heresy.

§ Sensitive and perceptive ministers tend to their congregations to keep them firmly in the faith.

§ Christian witness is a costly demand.

§ § § § § § §

Third Missionary Journey

Antioch (18:22)

Galatia and Phrygia (18:23)

Ephesus (18:24–19:41)

Macedonia and Greece (20:1-5)

Troas (20:6-12)

Miletus (20:13-38)

Jerusalem (21:1-16)

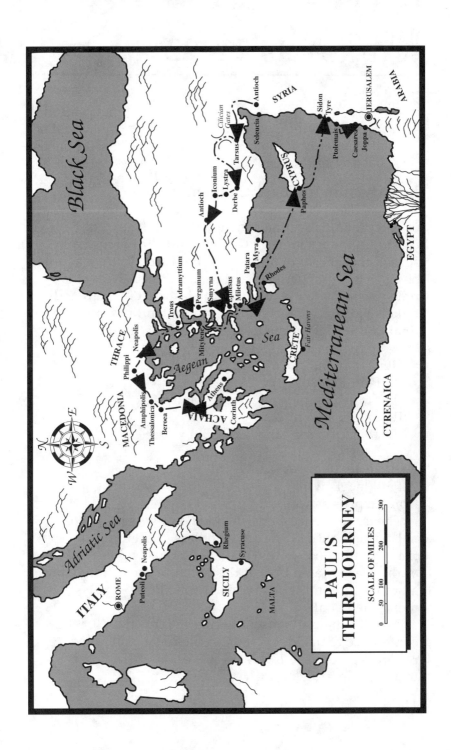

PAUL'S
THIRD JOURNEY

SCALE OF MILES

0 50 100 200 300

PART FIFTEEN Acts 21–22

Introduction to These Chapters

The previous section concluded with the end of Paul's third missionary journey (21:16). Paul's missions have spread the Christian message to both well-known and obscure places. Barriers have been hurdled. Now it is time to complete the work. In the last part of chapter 21, Luke's narrative gains momentum as Paul begins his final journey, this time to Rome itself.

Here is an outline of Acts 21:17–22:30:
  I. Paul in Jerusalem (21:17-26)
 II. More Trouble and Arrest (21:27-40)
III. Paul's Speech (22:1-21)
 IV. An Outraged Mob (22:22-30)

Paul in Jerusalem (21:17-26)

Paul meets with Mnason of Cyprus (Barnabas came from Cyprus as well).

The *we* reference comes to an end in verse 18, and does not resume until 27:1. Some scholars, therefore, suggest that the itinerary section ends here. Luke's presentation of the scene places Paul at the center of the action. James assumes little more than a silent role; Peter is not mentioned at all.

As with the previous gathering in Jerusalem for the conference to decide on the Gentile issue, a detailed report is given (see 15:12). However, no collection is mentioned in this narrative.

The tone of this discussion is extremely important. Are those in the congregation merely pleased at Paul's success? Or are they relieved that things are not as bad as they had thought?

In either event, the Christian congregation in Jerusalem has prospered, though these Christians are characterized as keeping the traditions of the law. It could be that they did not suffer persecution as did other Christians precisely because they did not distance themselves from what the rest of culture expected. If this is the case, then perhaps we can understand why the Jerusalem church is not as well remembered as the Antioch congregation. In Antioch Christians dared to be significantly different.

The conservative element still does not understand Paul. They suspect that he leads Jews to apostasy. Now if the leaders already know about Paul and fear his influence among Christians with strong ties to the traditions of Moses, what will happen when the rest of the Christians see Paul?

A moderate proposal is suggested. Paul will assist four needy Nazirites (see Numbers 6:1-21), thus showing his concern for the law.

Luke gives a reminder of the compromise that had been reached earlier (see 15:20).

Paul fulfills the Nazirite tradition of purity on the following day (see Joshua 3:5; 2 Chronicles 29:5, 34; 30:17). In his letter to the Corinthians (1 Corinthians 9:20), Paul speaks of his willingness to do whatever is necessary to bring people the Christian message. His acquiescence to the request of conservatives in Jerusalem gives substance to his claim.

More Trouble and Arrest (21:27-40)

After a full week during which Paul fulfills the tradition, there are still many who do not yet comprehend what Paul is doing. Still they charge him with apostasy. Since it is the Pentecost season, Paul is probably attacked by Jews who had gathered from around the empire (diaspora Jews).

Apostasy is itself bad enough, but Paul also commits a capital offense by bringing Greeks into the Temple in Jerusalem.

Quite predictably a riot breaks out. A few men create a disturbance by exaggerating the charges and haranguing the crowd, which has no sympathy for subtlety or examination of details. That the entire city is in an uproar may be an exaggeration, but enough of a disturbance erupts to alarm the Roman troops.

A cohort consists of about 760 infantry with a squadron attached. The troops were quartered in the citadel of Antonia. A small contingent is dispatched to prevent further beating. However, Paul ends up a prisoner of Roman authorities.

Luke uses the following exchange in order to illustrate two truths about the Christian movement. First, all of Palestine seethed under Roman occupation and control. Many nationalist movements wanted nothing less than the defeat of detested Roman rule. Periodically, uprisings did occur. By Paul's denial of any insurrectionist intent, the Roman authorities learn that Christianity is not a revolutionary movement in a political sense. The second point is similar to the first: Christianity is not a violent movement.

The Egyptian is Sicarii, who led an uprising during the rule of Felix. These revolutionaries stabbed their victims, from which practice the movement's name is derived. *Sica* means *dagger*. In another movement, some 30,000 soldiers had marched to seize Jerusalem. Recall that Gamaliel's counsel referred to Theudas (see 5:36). The real problem with Paul is that he appears to disturb the peace.

Paul does not mention his birthplace in his letter to the Philippians (see 3:5). Clearly, Paul is a well-educated man.

Paul's Speech (22:1-21)

Paul uses familiar terms in order to maintain his identity as a Jew. His use of Hebrew does the same. Stephen had done the same in his defense (see 7:2). At this time the high priest and the Sanhedrin are not present. They will be present later (23:1).

By his own account, Paul is still a Jew brought up within the strongest of Jewish laws and customs. Born outside Palestine (as many of the audience are; remember that at Pentecost Jews from all over the Roman Empire gathered in Jerusalem), he grew up in Jerusalem. Trained by Gamaliel, Paul is in the pharisaical tradition.

This Way means the Christian movement (see 9:2). Paul speaks as if the higher authorities—High Priest and Sanhedrin—are the same now as they were twenty years earlier (see 9:1; 26:12).

In the previous account the time of day is not given, though people rarely traveled at night (see 10:9).

In verse 7 Luke adds *Jesus of Nazareth* (see 9:4-5). In 9:7 Paul's companions hear the voice but do not see the light, the opposite of what he says here.

Luke maintains the close linkage with Judaism by describing Ananias as a devout man who is respected by his fellows in Damascus. Verses 12 and following are the same as 9:10-17.

The God of our fathers (NIV) or *ancestors* (NRSV) sustains the strong Jewish tradition. *The Righteous One* is also alluded to in 3:14; 7:52; 1 John 2:1.

Witnessing to all men echoes 9:15 and 26:16-18. The mission to the Gentiles will be specified in verse 21. Baptism is done with the invocation of Jesus' name (see 2:38), and sins are washed away (see 1 Corinthians 6:11; Ephesians 5:26).

Paul's strong affiliation with Judaism is once again emphasized by his prayer in the Temple. In this holy place Paul saw the vision, though he does not use the name of Jesus in this description. Paul left Jerusalem at the Lord's instruction, not because of a Jewish plot (however, compare 9:29).

Without provocation Paul confesses his earlier persecution. Surely Jews will listen another Jew who was persecuted; but they will not.

Stephen is described as a martyr. Though in chapter 9 persecution erupts when Stephen dies, here his death seems to be the culmination of persecution. The Gentile mission has been directed all along by Jesus (see 9:15).

In no sense has Paul responded to the charges that caused his arrest in the first place. He makes no mention of bringing a Greek into the Temple. What, then, is Luke's purpose in using this long speech?

The problem of the relationship between Jews and Christians is not a new problem. Evidently during Luke's life the same problem caused considerable controversy. Luke uses Paul's speech to show how closely the two perspectives are related. Christians are more open to the mission to the Gentiles and willing to receive them by baptism.

Had Paul repudiated his Jewish past, Christians might in some sense be justified in rejecting all that Judaism is. But Paul—and, by implication, Luke—does not reject the rich Jewish tradition.

An Outraged Mob (22:22-30)

Paul's description of Stephen's stoning (verses 17-21) brings another surge of anger (see Acts 2:14) and Paul finds himself in the same peril he was in earlier (see 21:36). Luke's description is of a mob in an absolutely furious rage. Evidently they know nothing of the compromise that had been won in the earlier debate. Decisions by councils do not end prejudice in people.

Scourging is a form of torture used on slaves and non-Roman citizens. The man is stripped and has his hands tied to a post. Sometimes the beating would be with a whip. Occasionally the straps had pieces of metal or bone to make the torture worse. Death by scourging was not uncommon.

Only when he has been bent over the bench does Paul speak of his rights as a citizen. A false claim of citizenship is punishable by death.

Luke includes the detail of a purchased citizenship in order to emphasize Paul's citizenship by right of birth. The torture does not happen, but by the same token polite conversation ends. The tribune has come too close to violating a Roman law against murder.

This incident is the first of many in which Roman authority finds no evidence to convict Paul, and, by implication, Christianity. (Other similar incidents occur in 24:22-23; 25:18-22; 26:31-32.) Luke does not stress the same theme with equal emphasis throughout Acts. He stresses the Roman tolerance in these final chapters of the dramatic confrontation between Paul and higher authorities.

The chapter concludes with the scene of the following day. The tribune wants clarification as to why Paul has been accused. This time the high priest and the Sanhedrin are in attendance.

§ § § § § § §

The Message of Acts 21–22

Paul returns from his missionary journey with great successes to report. However, the hard-won compromise of the Jerusalem Conference seems nearly forgotten by some and unknown by many more. The same question emerges again: What is the appropriate relationship with the Gentiles? Luke also uses Paul's defense to speak to Christians about another dilemma: the relationship between Christians and Jews.

What can we learn from these chapters?

§ Paul's intention is to get to Jerusalem and then to Rome. From the outsider's perspective his arrest implies failure. But God will use this circumstance to get Paul to Rome. The eyes of faith can see God at work even in seemingly unexplainable events.

§ Paul can adapt to different expectations without losing his own integrity.

§ Christians cannot forget their Jewish heritage without some loss of their own identity as people of biblical faith.

§ Paul's genius is that he understands God's love for all people. This truth offends any who want God to love only their own kind.

§ Under pressure Paul maintains his integrity.

§ The Christian witness may have to survive not only in the face of a hostile, screaming mob, but within familiar settings of friends who do not understand the vast implications of God's intention.

§ § § § § § §

Acts 23–24

Introduction to These Chapters

Luke's work in earlier chapters spans large amounts of time and great distances. In the later chapters, especially those discussing Paul's appearance and defense to the Roman authorities, Luke takes the time to include detail. The sense of drama is increased as is the implication that Paul and Christianity pose no real threat to the Roman authorities.

In these two chapters Paul appears before both Jewish authorities (the Sanhedrin) and Roman authorities. He has sharp dissent with Jews but little conflict that is against Rome.

Here is an outline of Acts 23 and 24:
  I. Paul's Defense (23:1-11)
 II. A Plot Develops (23:12-15)
III. Paul Is Removed from the Scene (23:16-35)
 IV. Paul Is Charged (24:1-9)
  V. Paul's Response (24:10-23)
 VI. The Verdict Is Delayed (24:24-27)

Paul's Defense (23:1-11)

The previous chapter closes with the scene shifting to the following day. The tribune wants clarification (see 21:34).

Paul confronts the Sanhedrin without fear either of the Sanhedrin or of God. He has a clear conscience (see 1 Timothy 1:5; 2 Timothy 1:3; 1 Peter 3:16, 21).

The high priest Ananias was assassinated around A.D. 66. Here the Old Testament curse is used as a prophecy (see Deuteronomy 28:22).

In this speech Paul does not appear antagonistic towards the law. Luke takes great pains to show clearly that Paul has not arbitrarily renounced his entire tradition.

The major theological understanding of resurrection offers Paul a means by which to split his opposition. That he holds this belief may indicate Paul's own pharisaical background. In any event, he certainly implies the resurrection of Jesus. Predictably, the assembly erupts in theological debate.

Pharisees believe in resurrection, Spirit, and angels. Sadducees hold to none of these tenets. Clearly, then, the Sadducees cannot tolerate Paul's assertion that he had been addressed by the Spirit (see 22:7).

The tribune, having sought clarification, now fears violence. In the moment of greatest peril Paul has yet another vision of Christ (see 16:9; 18:9-10; 27:23). This remarkable episode illustrates Luke's desire to show the affinity between Christianity and Judaism. Both Christian and Jew share similar theological understandings: resurrection, Spirit, and angels. Furthermore, since all Judaism is not alike, the Christian does not have to completely sever relationships with people or tradition. This subtle message would not be lost on Luke's readers.

A Plot Develops (23:12-15)

Since the previous night's meeting does not result in Paul's immediate conviction, a plot develops among some Jews. Forty fanatics are committed to kill Paul, but obviously they are not in the same barracks that house Roman garrison troops. Scribes are not mentioned in the plot; however, we cannot be certain that only the Sanhedrin is involved in the plot. The priest needs to give support.

Paul Is Removed from the Scene (23:16-35)

Luke is not concerned with the details of how Paul's nephew hears of the plot. Incredibly, Paul gives orders to the soldier. Even more incredibly, the soldier obeys.

The tribune ascertains the nature of the plot. At the same time, the conspirators have come to an agreement as to the timing of the attempt. Fully aware of the imminent danger now, the tribune takes charge of the situation.

The scene changes to the Roman preparations to protect their prisoner. Two centurions command some 200 men. Seventy horsemen will accompany the troops. Two hundred other men (either bowmen or bodyguards) will march as well. The entire company will depart between 9:00 and 10:00 P.M. Paul is provided with a mount as well.

Antonias Felix is the procurator of Judea. The letter from Claudis Lysias uses the same form of address that Luke uses in addressing Theophilus (see Luke 1:3). The letter implies that the Sanhedrin is being taken seriously. Some commentators suggest that the tribune has not presented the entire truth. But Luke's purpose is to show clearly that the Roman authorities have respected Paul from the outset, due to his citizenship.

Verse 27 corresponds to Paul's defense, though the speech itself is left out. The Roman understanding is that the conflict between Paul and the Sanhedrin is little more than a theological argument.

Finally the reason for Paul's nighttime removal is explained. The conspirators will be able to present their case at a later time.

Antipatris is some forty miles away, a rather long march for foot soldiers. The mounted troops deliver Paul to Caesarea, about twenty-five miles distant. Felix begins making arrangements for a hearing, presumably to be held when the conspirators arrive. Hearings could be held in one of three places: (1) the accused's province (for

Paul this would mean Cilicia); (2) the province of the crime itself; or (3) the province in which the accused had been captured.

Luke's readers would have recognized immediately that this is the third time Roman authorities have rescued Paul (see 21:32 when Paul is in the Temple, and 23:10 when he is in the presence of the Sanhedrin). Roman authority has been benevolent from the beginning of this drama—ever since Paul's citizenship is established as valid. On the other hand, the Jewish authorities are very antagonistic towards Paul, and even become involved in a plot to end his life. Recall that Luke's readers would have seen an immediate parallel between the peril of Paul and the passion of Jesus when Jewish authorities conspired against him.

The drama is now set. What will happen to Paul?

Paul Is Charged (24:1-9)

A five-day interval passes before the arrival of the conspirators.

Tertullus is familiar with both Roman and Jewish law. The entire delegation presents the case against Paul.

Felix is known for his cruelty. He had many freedom fighters crucified in order to eliminate resistance and revolt. Ironically, his attitude in this incident seems to be one of benevolence. The expression of peace stretches the truth. Tertullus knows how to speak graciously to those in power. He follows the classic rhetorical style. The concluding sentence in the introduction to the speech is an overly polite phrase.

The speech of Tertullus echoes the accusations against Jesus (see Luke 23:2). Luke thus illustrates the parallel between what befalls Paul and what Jesus endured in his passion. Christians would make the association very quickly.

The term *sect* is used here in derogatory fashion (see 4:12; 28:22). Nazarenes is the term used to describe followers of Jesus (see 2:22). It is clear that the charges are exaggerated in order to show Paul as a threat to Roman authority because he is a political revolutionary and ringleader. In no sense are the charges true, but they are being molded to fit the conspirator's wishes and intentions. Even the charge of violating the Temple is inserted.

The NRSV and the NIV delete verse 7. The reason is that this verse, when it is inserted, implies that Lysias rather than Paul is the antecedent of *him* in verse 8.

The charges are clear. The governor will be able to determine for himself whether they are true after his examination of Paul.

Paul's Response (24:10-23)

The word *defense* is critical in the later chapters of Acts. Luke counts only the days spent in Jerusalem: Paul's arrival (21:17); his negotiations with James and the elders on the second day (21:18); days three through nine spent in purification (21:27); his appearance before the Sanhedrin on the tenth day (22:30); on day eleven, his discovery of the plot to kill him (23:12); and his transfer to Caesarea on the twelfth day (23:32). Luke's intention is to show a devout Jewish man on his way to the Holy City for the celebration of a Jewish festival. Up to this time Paul has not deliberately stirred up any controversy.

Paul finally answers the charges leveled in verse 5. Tertullus' charges cannot be proven. Paul then makes an accounting of himself in the Christian way (see 9:2 in which *the Way* is referred to with the same connotations as *sect* is in this encounter). Paul uses terms which evoke memories of Old Testament heritage: God of the fathers, the Law, and the Prophets.

Without specifically mentioning a messiah, Paul does include the hope of resurrection for both Christians and Jews.

Judgment is bound up with resurrection, and therefore, Paul strives to have a clear conscience.

Alms (NRSV) or *gifts for the poor* refer to the collection for the famine-racked land.

If disturbances are to be blamed on anyone, then the blame should be on the Jews who stirred up the trouble in the first place. And since eyewitnesses are not present, Paul's guilt cannot be proven. Paul then turns to address or gesture to his accusers. Again, his pharisaic background includes hope in the resurrection, so he is quite within the bounds of Jewish orthodoxy.

We do not know how Felix could have learned anything about the Christian movement. But Luke uses this knowledge as a means by which to arrive at adjournment, keeping Paul in custody.

Commentators point out that this defense differs from others in Acts. Here Paul engages his accusers in conversation. After the Jewish charges are delivered through the spokesman Tertullus—Paul as instigator of revolt and violator of the Temple—Paul responds. The defense includes traditions which link Christianity and Judaism. Rather than desecrating the Temple, Paul goes there as a pilgrim with an offering. Clearly the new faith is not merely an out-of-hand rejection of all that has come before it.

The Verdict Is Delayed (24:24-27)

Drusilla is the daughter of Agrippa I, born about A.D. 38. She is the sister of Agrippa II and Bernice (see 25:13). She was first engaged to Antiochus Epiphanes of Commogene and then married to King Aziz of Emessa. She exhibits real interest in the Christian faith.

The central tenets in early Christian preaching are listed. All of them would have been offensive to Felix, who has incestuous relations with his sister. Even though Luke does not include the story of John the Baptist confronting Herod, this story obviously parallels that famous challenge.

Since Felix brings up the possibility of a bribe, many think that this refers to the offering Paul carries with him.

A period of two years passes as Paul remains a prisoner. Thus Luke shows for the second time Roman witness to the innocence of the Christian apostle. As a matter of fact, the Roman appears interested in the movement and is nearly converted. (Recall a similar incident in 13:7-12 with Sergius Paulus.) But the central focus is still on the trial and Paul's plight.

§ § § § § § §

The Message of Acts 23–24

With increased attention to detail, Luke presents a dramatic development. The apostle Paul now faces the attack of both the official authority (the Sanhedrin) and unofficial resistance (a conspiracy to kill him). Luke shows Roman concern for the safety of a citizen and a tacit tolerance for the Christian movement. In no way do Roman authorities feel threatened by the Christians. The entire challenge to Christianity comes from Jewish leaders. And within Christianity itself, as represented by Paul, there is an important link between Jewish tradition and theology and the Christian hope and ethic.

What can we learn from these chapters?

§ The Christian needs to understand the biblical roots of faith.

§ Opponents will sometimes bend the truth in order to corner the faithful.

§ A clear conscience is critical when challenged by evil intent.

§ The Christian does not have to grovel at the feet of authority; the Christian is bound by and trusts in higher authority.

§ Christians are not revolutionaries bent on the destruction of existing government.

§ Christians and Jews share a great deal of heritage and hope.

§ God sustains the faithful in moments of great stress.

§ § § § § § §

Acts 25–26

Introduction to These Chapters

When reading Luke's narrative of the dramatic events surrounding Paul's defense before both Jewish and Roman authorities we may be tempted to rush quickly on to find out what the results are. How does this end? What happens next? Such questions indicate the skill with which Luke presents the material. And we are involved in the reading. But we must consciously slow ourselves down sufficiently to ask what Luke is attempting to show or illustrate through these thrilling narratives. What is the purpose of the stories?

In the previous chapter, for instance, Paul has a vision of Christ at a particularly stressful moment. How would the apostle continue his work? Would he finally get to his destination? Was there sufficient resistance that the work of God could be stopped? Not only Paul but Christian readers as well must wrestle with these questions. Chapters 25 and 26 now continue the drama. Will the encouragement Paul received be enough? For how long can Christians anticipate Roman authority to treat them benevolently? What will happen if the Roman benevolence ends?

One more question emerges. What attitude does the writer have toward Roman authority in this narrative? Luke's presentation clearly shows a benevolent attitude toward Roman rule. In no small measure, Luke presses this significant point home to his readers, whether they be Christian or Roman.

Here is an outline of Acts 25 and 26:

The Arrival of Festus (25:1-5)

The new governor, Festus, makes a visit to his new assignment as soon as possible. At his arrival the trial proceedings are set into motion once again. The chief priest is Ishmael, son of Phabi. Again the charges are presented, though here the entire body presents them. In 24:1 they are presented by only a small number.

Rather than risk Paul's assassination on the journey, Festus decides to make the trip himself.

Luke's presentation makes the Romans appear almost reluctant to continue the trial. Under no circumstances do Romans conspire with Jews against the Christians.

Paul's Appearance in Court (25:6-12)

The scene shifts to Caesarea and the trial. We hear of the charges only through Paul's response. Recall that a similar reversal had occurred earlier when we heard of the influence of Paul's preaching through the words of Demetrius in Ephesus. Now we hear Paul.

Two of the three charges are familiar. Paul has not broken Jewish law (see 21:21), nor has he broken Temple law (see 21:28). But he adds another defense: He has not broken Caesar's law. Is this a new accusation of sedition or revolt? Has Festus decided to acquiesce to the Jewish demand? Or does he plan to get more eyewitnesses in order to acquit Paul?

Paul's appeal to Caesar troubles scholars. Paul seems

much more concerned with his rights than with his life. The entire undertaking has become a matter of principle. The Christian movement will not hide in the corner to be drawn out by force. Nor will the movement gently concede to intimidation. Paul's citizenship has been authenticated by his word (see 22:27). When is appeal allowed? Before sentencing? After sentencing? One thing is certain, Paul is under great stress and makes his appeal in reaction to both the Sanhedrin and the procurator.

Festus gives an early indication of his benevolent attitude. Still, the tension remains. What will happen to Paul?

A Defense of Christianity (25:13-27)

The scene shifts again. An indefinite amount of time passes. Agrippa II is the great-grandson of Herod the Great, born A.D. 27, died about A.D. 100. Bernice is Agrippa's sister, about one year younger.

The entire case is now presented to Agrippa. Luke's readers also have a recounting of the drama. The Roman authorities are proceeding according to the letter of the law. Christianity is getting excellent treatment under Roman law.

The Jerusalem scene is vividly recreated. The Jews demand Paul's condemnation from the outset. The entire council, chief priest and elders, intensify the accusation. But Roman authority does not easily give in, even to such persistent and dramatic demands.

Against the intense hostility of the Jews, Roman ignorance shows sharply. Luke here presents officials who are trained in Roman law and tradition and can make no sense of the Jewish concern. The Resurrection, in particular, seems little more than a superstition (here used to describe religion).

Festus omits the suspicion of an assassination plot. The appeal is self-evident in Paul's request. Luke concludes the scene in a way remarkably like the Passion narrative of Jesus. In the Passion Jesus faces the sinister coalition of political and religious forces. Here Paul faces the same perilous collaboration. For the time being, however, his end is not so clear.

The following scene takes place amidst royal trappings and flourishes. But the attention is not on royalty as much as it is on Paul, who stands in the middle of it all. Where others may have felt intimidated by such authority, Paul appears unflinching.

The long speech of Festus enlarges the number of Jews who want Paul dead. Now all of them do. The tone of the assertion recalls the mob scenes (see 21:36; 22:22). Judaism, not Roman authority, attacks Christianity, according to Luke's presentation. Once again, Roman rulers do not have sufficient evidence to prosecute the Christian.

The entire scene portrays Paul, and therefore Christianity, in the very center of the public eye. The movement is not conspiring in the dark or in the shadows. It does not shrink from public examination. Luke's purpose seems to be to show just how public the Christian movement is.

Other individuals have no doubt appeared before the royal assembly, but they may have been rendered almost incoherent with fear. After all, who can stand before Roman authority without fear? Luke's point is that the Christian can, for two reasons. The first is that God will be present, as when people were in prison and God was there. Secondly, the Christian knows the authority of the higher calling, the authority of God that must be obeyed.

Paul's Defense (26:1-25)

Paul makes an eloquent defense for himself. In no manner does Paul hint that the Romans should be concerned. His defense will have to do only with Jewish charges.

Even though the appeal depends upon Paul's

citizenship, he makes no reference to Tarsus. His entire background is pharisaical and in Jerusalem (see 22:3). The theological hope of resurrection links the past with the present. Paul contends that he is on trial for his belief in the Resurrection. The implication is, of course, that God has raised Jesus from the dead. The Jews simply cannot accept this concept.

Paul's entire presentation has attempted to show the strong link between Jews and Christians. Now he shifts his argument to describe his own experience. This description begins the third and final recounting of Paul's conversion. Luke's literary style is very important here. By using three occasions to recount the dramatic events on the road to Damascus, Luke has indicated how important the conversion is in the life of the church.

To begin with, Paul confesses guilt for the deaths of many Christians, not just one (Stephen in 8:1). Even in the synagogues Paul persecuted people.

Slight differences in detail occur in this account of Paul's conversion (see 9:3 and 22:5). Luke adds variety, lest it become dull repetition. But alteration of detail does not alter the substance of the dramatic event. The intensity of the light is even greater in this account. In 9:4 only Paul falls to the ground. The others see nothing. In 22:6, Paul is struck down.

Kick against the goads is a common Greek saying which means that opposition is senseless and impossible.

God's command to Paul to stand on his feet is reminiscent of Ezekiel's call (see Ezekiel 2:1).

The promise of deliverance has been a consistent one (7:10, 34; 12:6-10; see also Jeremiah 1:7-8; 1 Chronicles 16:35).

Open their eyes picks up a theme from the servant songs of Isaiah (Isaiah 42:7, 16).

The implication is now made clear. Paul could not disobey the authority of God through Christ. Paul gives a name to the higher authority that he and other Christians must obey. Thus the Christian mission is justified.

Paul's work is preaching, which he has done in Damascus (see 9:19-22) and Jerusalem (see 9:28-29). Christian preaching calls for repentance and change. Remarkably, Paul has changed the charges that have been brought against him. According to his witness, his preaching, not the violation of the Temple, has brought about the present crisis (see 21:28).

Summarizing his work, Paul once again draws attention to the consistency of the Christian hope with the work of Moses and the prophets. Throughout it all God has been with Paul (the promise of verse 17 is fulfilled).

The basic tenets of Christian faith are then sketched out. The suffering messiah has been foretold in the Old Testament. He would be raised and thus proclaim light to the world (see Isaiah 9:1-2).

A Lively Exchange (26:24-32)

Festus' interruption draws attention to these basic beliefs, especially of resurrection. He can only scoff at the suggestion. Against his scoffing, Paul appears serious and completely unintimidated by the ruler.

Agrippa, being a Jew, is called on as a witness. But he refuses to become involved in the theological debate. We cannot tell exactly what tone his comment to Paul takes. But he at least gives a nod of assent to the courageous Christian.

In verse 29, Luke has a character glance out at the reader/observer, thus indicating the reader in the action of the story. When Paul declares that he wishes that all could be Christian, Luke's readers no doubt pray the same wish.

Paul has had the last word. The Roman authorities can find nothing worth punishment. But the appeal binds Paul to a journey to Rome.

Once again we must remember that Luke is not only recounting a tense encounter. He is also using the narrative to illustrate a further point. The intensity of Paul's persecution is greater in this account than the previous two. Therefore the conversion illustrates the greater power of Christ.

Luke also uses the narrative to show the relationship among the three interests. The Jews are his mortal enemies. Roman rule, on the other hand, seems benevolent. Luke could be preparing Christians to live in the Roman Empire. Moreover, Rome can trust the Christian movement in the empire since the Christians are neither a secret society (26:26) nor subversive.

§ § § § § § §

The Message of Acts 25–26

The scenes of Paul's trial are at once both thrilling and terrifying. The grandeur of royalty, the flourish and trappings of imperial government, and the authority of Rome all appear very intimidating. In the midst of all this stands a single figure with little more than the authority of his conversion, the summons to mission, and his experience in the mission field. Yet, through it all, Luke has little question about how events will turn out. The promise of God's presence is no vague or empty hope. God is sufficient for the hour and present in the need of the moment. With this assurance firmly in mind, the Christian can withstand even the most demanding trials.

What else can we learn from these chapters?

§ The Christian is concerned with responsibilities, and does not necessarily protect reputation or status.

§ The Christian's calling has the authority of God behind it.

§ The truth of Christ's resurrection will confuse many; but nevertheless it must be proclaimed.

§ In the midst of stress, an individual will draw on what is internalized—what is known to be true in personal experience.

§ The act of conversion affects the balance of a person's life, and may take the Christian to places she or he does not want to go.

§ Christianity trusts in the power and promise of God and is therefore not off in a corner, shrinking from the trouble in the world.

§ § § § § § §

Acts 27–28

Introduction to These Chapters

Chapters 27 and 28 bring the Christian message at long
last to Rome, though in a manner different from what
Paul had anticipated at the beginning. Luke's narrative
has maintained suspense for quite some time now. Trials,
narrow escapes, and confrontations all threaten to
overwhelm Paul. But God has protected the movement's
main spokesman.

In the final narrative Paul takes a perilous journey to
Rome. The narrative itself is one of the longest in the
entire Bible. It compares with the length and character of
the Joseph story in Genesis 37–50.

Here is an outline of Acts 27 and 28:
  I. The Journey Begins (27:1-8)
 II. Bad Omens (27:9-12)
III. Storm, Drifting, and Landfall (27:13-44)
 IV. On Malta (28:1-6)
  V. A Miraculous Healing (28:7-10)
 VI. From Malta to Rome (28:11-16)
VII. In Rome (28:17-31)

The Journey Begins (27:1-8)

A unit called the Augustan Cohort is stationed in the
area. The home port of the ship is Adramyttium, which is
a city southeast of Troas. Aristarchus is mentioned by

Paul in two of his letters (see Philemon 24; Colossians 4:10).

The Roman commander treats Paul very well during the journey. Paul is given freedom to visit with friends, perhaps during the loading of cargo.

A direct voyage to Italy cannot be made. To begin with, the ships are cargo vessels and have to work the various ports along the way. The season is not good for travel, since it is a winter voyage. *Under* (NRSV) refers to the *lee* (NIV) side of Cyprus, the east side.

The coastal current moves westerly, thus making the voyage possible. At night the breeze shifts and comes off the land.

The *we* reference gives the impression of an eyewitness report of the activities surrounding the travelers. Evidently the centurion is responsible for securing passage on whatever vessels he can find. In this instance he has found a ship transporting grain from Egypt to Rome.

Large cargo vessels have only one large sail. Therefore, tacking across the wind is impossible. The ship has to sail with the wind. The route takes them from Myra to Rhodes, then on toward Crete. They will pass on the lee side of Crete by Cape Salmone. Fair Havens, also called Good Harbor, is near the city of Lasea.

Bad Omens (27:9-12)

Evidently a great deal of time has elapsed and the late summer departure has turned into a very hazardous winter journey. Travel by sea is usually halted between mid-November and mid-March. We can date this narrative by the fifth day before the Atonement (*Yom Kippur*), October 5, in the year A.D. 59.

Reminiscent of the voyage of Jonah, dire predictions are made about shipwreck and catastrophe.

Luke emphasizes the centurion's authority by showing him to have more than he really would have had. He could claim space for the entourage, but he would not have had authority over the technical questions of seafaring. Paul also shows knowledge of seafaring. However, Luke's purpose is to show Paul with the gift of prophetic foresight.

Phoenix is modern-day Phineka.

Storm, Drifting, and Landfall (27:13-44)

A favorable wind allows for a short voyage to change harbors. But the wind shifts, forcing the ship off course. By using a smaller sail the ship manages to avoid disaster.

For a short time the ship enjoys a respite from the terrifying storm. The boat is probably a small lifeboat.

Syrtis is an especially dangerous region with sandbanks that threaten shipping.

When the storm threatens to sink the vessel, all extra gear is jettisoned (see Jonah 1:5). Three days later some of the ship's necessities are pitched overboard as well.

Luke brings the scene to a climax with the vessel now at the mercy of the sea. The story itself will continue in verse 27. For the moment Luke leaves his readers wondering about the fate of Paul and the beleaguered crew.

Paul assumes the stance of an orator (recall a similar technique in 17:22, on Mars Hill). Why does Luke interrupt the dramatic narrative? He wants to show that Paul, the center figure, is remarkably calm in dire circumstances. He trusts God's promise that God will remain with the imperiled apostle.

All on board are seasick and do not eat. Only later, in verse 26, do the sailors finally eat.

The appearance of an angel requires no further explanation to either Jewish or Gentile thinking. The divine sign clearly insures Paul's safe arrival in Rome to give witness to the Christian faith. The entire crew and passengers will be saved as well as Paul. Paul reiterates his hope and trust in God's protection and guidance.

Malta is the only island within 250 miles of Tunisia and Sicily.

After Paul expresses his trust in God, the narrative picks up again from where it stopped at verse 20. The vessel has been adrift for two weeks.

Luke heightens the drama by detailing the sailors' actions upon sighting land. They check the depth of the water; the vessel is approaching land very rapidly. Numerous anchors are used to prevent the vessel from being turned broadside to the waves by the wind. What follows is a very confused picture. Sailors surely would not leave the relative safety of the vessel for the unknown of a crashing surf. Soldiers mistrust the sailors.

Through it all Paul is pictured as keeping faithful watch, even though he is a novice at seafaring. To compound the crisis, the soldiers cut the lifeboat loose. Now the larger vessel will have to be beached.

After a terrifying night Paul reassures the sailors of their ultimate safety. The reference to the hairs on their heads is similar to words from the Gospels (see Luke 21:18).

Luke's readers would have recognized immediately the image of the Eucharist/Communion with the blessing and breaking of bread. Perhaps Luke is implying that Christians should always give thanks, even in the midst of the most threatening circumstances.

Estimates differ as to the number of passengers on the ship. The Revised Standard Version reading is 276, though some authorities suggest only 76.

Since the storm has abated the vessel's hold can now be opened. Extra wheat is jettisoned into the sea.

The unrecognized land is probably modern-day St. Paul's Bay.

The lightened vessel is then steered along until it strikes the shoals, where it breaks apart.

Chained prisoners would have been little threat to armed soldiers. But Luke's purpose is to show the

Christian missionary in the worst possible circumstances. The benevolent protection of the centurion shines all the more brightly against the dark intentions of the others.

Luke shows little concern for details of how people made it safely to shore. His purpose has been fulfilled. The imperiled Christian missionary, having recently escaped from an assassination plot as well as many confrontations with Roman authority, now escapes from the storm-tossed sea. Paul does mention a shipwreck in his letter to the Corinthians (2 Corinthians 11:25).

On Malta (28:1-6)

The promise of Acts 27:26 is fulfilled; the ship's crew and passengers are safe on an island. The island's population consists of non-Greeks who speak a Semitic language. Veterans of Caesar's Roman armies also live on the island. The gathering around the fire is probably restricted to Christians, since all 276 people could not gather in a small area. The setting prepares the reader for the scene that follows.

As if the previous weeks of danger were not enough, the apostle is bitten by a poisonous snake. The natives are convinced, based on a tradition of their own, that justice has finally caught up with Paul. But he remains unharmed (see Matthew 16:18; Luke 10:19). Previously Paul refused to have any identification with the divine; here he does not correct the natives.

A Miraculous Healing (28:7-10)

In addition to the story of the serpent, Luke tells the story of a miraculous healing that occurs on the island. Again, Paul is the center of attention. *Publius* is the term for the local high official on the island.

Paul is still the wonder-worker through the laying on of hands. Even while a prisoner on the way to Rome, long besieged by enemies and tossed by the storm, Paul is still a man of great power. Luke's purpose in part is to retrieve for Paul a position of high status. We certainly have a different picture of Paul in Acts from the one we have in the revelations of his personal letters.

The gifts are possibly fees, but they are more likely a means by which to honor Paul.

From Malta to Rome (28:11-16)

After a three-month winter wait, the prisoner continues toward Rome in a vessel that had spent the winter in a safe harbor. *Twin brothers* (NRSV) or *gods* (NIV) means Castor and Pollux, who were worshiped by sailors.

Either the wind conditions or the need to unload cargo holds the ship in Syracuse for three days.

Rhegium is modern Reggio Calabria. Puteoli is on the Gulf of Naples, about two days' journey from Malta with favorable winds. The Appian Way to Rome is five days' journey.

On the way the travelers visit with other Christians. Note the recurrent theme that Christian congregations exist all around the empire. These anonymous communities continue God's work. This is the only reference to Roman Christians in the entire book of Acts.

The Forum of Appius is forty-three miles away, and Three Taverns is some thirty-three miles away. Both sites are on the Appian Way.

We no longer appears as of verse 16. Nor are Roman authorities mentioned. Finally Paul reaches Rome at the pinnacle of his career as a missionary. The gospel has been spread even to the center of the empire. Paul lives in private housing while being guarded by soldiers.

In Rome (28:17-31)

Paul summons the Jewish leadership, presbyters, rulers, synagogue officials, and patrons (see 25:2; Luke 19:47).

In his address Paul exonerates himself of any blame.

He has done nothing against the Jews (see 26:19-20), nor has he violated tradition (see 21:21; 24:5). Yet he is still in Roman hands. If it were up to the Romans he would be released. But he has appealed to Caesar, and this is a major charge. The Sanhedrin is not even mentioned.

Paul's hope, the Christian hope, is for the Messiah. *Chain* can mean either real chains that bound him, or figuratively, his being compelled to witness.

Evidently the stir in Jerusalem has not yet reached Rome. The people know nothing of the reports about Paul. They want to know what his views are about this Christian movement, or *sect*, that has been widely attacked.

Paul's preaching continues to express the central truths of the faith: the kingdom of God; the person of Jesus, his death, and the resurrection promised in Scripture and fulfilled in Jesus. The results are predictable. They do not believe, and they disagree among themselves.

Isaiah 6:9-10 is quoted as explanation of Jewish rejection of Jesus (see Matthew 13:14-15; Mark 4:12). The tragedy is that Jews have rejected the Christian hope and claim.

Luke then returns to one of the major themes throughout this book. Salvation is sent to the Gentiles (see 13:48). The Jews' rejection of the message helped provoke the missions to the Gentiles.

Paul remains for two years under house arrest. The visitors probably are Gentiles. As in earlier episodes in Pisidian Antioch (13:46) and Corinth (18:6), Jews reject the gospel and Gentiles accept it.

Paul's death is assumed but not described. In earlier speeches Paul had indicated that he would suffer a martyr's death (see 27:24).

The book ends on a triumphant note. The gospel is proclaimed unhindered. Rome's tolerance continues.

§ § § § § § §

The Message of Acts 27–28

Luke's original readers would have realized very quickly that the extended narrative is intended to heighten the drama of Paul and the Christian hope. Through is all God proves faithful to the promise that the intention of God cannot be discouraged. God would see to it that the message is proclaimed even in Rome. Triumph is implicit throughout. But along with triumph is the tragedy that many who hear the gospel continue to reject it.

Luke's primary feeling is that of loss. Modern Christian readers should be careful that a reading of the book of Acts does not feed the fires of anti-Jewish feeling. As Luke has shown very deliberately and carefully, Christians and Jews share a tremendous heritage. They also share a wonderful hope that God continues to press for the divine purpose to succeed unhindered throughout the whole of creation.

What else can we learn from Acts 27 and 28?

§ God's intention can be delayed, but not denied altogether.

§ God can and will use different persons to accomplish the divine purposes. In this narrative, even detested soldiers are used to protect the Christian missionary.

§ Rejection of the gospel is not the final word.

§ Rejection in Acts merely opens up new territory for the gospel message.

§ § § § § § §

Glossary of Terms

Achaia: Roman province comprising most of ancient Greece south of Macedonia. Corinth was the administrative center. During Paul's time the Roman proconsul was Gallio (18:12).

Agabus: The prophet who predicted widespread famine (11:28). He spoke with a special gift from the Spirit. Later he predicted that Paul would be bound over to the Romans (21:10-11).

Agrippa II: Marcus Julius Agrippa (A.D. 27–100). Had Jewish interests but clearly preferred Roman ways. His relationship with his sister was merely scandalous.

Ananias: A Christian in Jerusalem who conspired with his wife Sapphira to hold back a portion of property. When confronted separately each died (5:1, 3, 5). Also, a Christian disciple who helped Paul in Damascus (chapter 9). Also, a Jewish high priest before whom Paul appeared at the end of the third missionary journey (23:2).

Antioch: Hellenistic city in northwest Syria. Ranked with Rome and Alexandria as a major center. Early center for Christian expansion. It was in Antioch that followers of Christ were first known as Christians (11:26).

Antioch of Pisidia: A city in the lake district of southwest Asia Minor. Sometimes called Pisidian Antioch (13:14). Paul preached here to a congregation of Jews and Greek-speaking Gentiles during the first journey.

Areopagus: A hill of nearly 400-foot elevation in Athens, also called Mars Hill. Also the name of the council that met here. Paul spoke to this council when challenged in Athens.

Artemis: A goddess of fertility for all living things worshipped in Ephesus and throughout Asia, even as far as Rome. The image associated with her is a meteorite (19:35). The shrines made by Demetrius are probably miniature sanctuaries.

Athens: The capital of modern Greece. It is the major city of the ancient district of Attica. The name is derived from the goddess Athena. Paul spoke here but he did not establish a Christian congregation.

Bartholomew: One of the twelve apostles, according to each of the four lists (Matthew 10:3; Mark 3:18; Luke 6:14; Acts 1:13). Traditionally a missionary to many countries.

Bernice: The daughter of Agrippa I. Married first to Marcus. When he died she was betrothed to Marcus' brother Herod. Had incestuous relationship with her brother, Agrippa II.

Caesar: The family of Julius Caesar. The name became the title as well. Caesar Augustus appears in Luke 2:1; as a title it appears twenty-seven times in the New Testament.

Caesarea: City on the coast of Palestine twenty-three miles from Mt. Carmel.

Caesarea Philippi: City on the southwest slope of Mt. Hermon; here Jesus questioned the disciples regarding his identity. Peter replied that Jesus was the Christ (Mark 8:27).

Cenchreae: A seaport seven miles east of Corinth on the Aegean Sea. In this city Paul cut his hair in accordance with Jewish tradition (Acts 18:18; also Romans 16:1).

Claudius: Fourth Roman emperor. His full name was Tiberius Claudius Nero Germanius. His reign extended from A.D. 41–54. Named in Acts 11:28 and 18:2; probably identified as Caesar in Acts 17:7.

Cohort: A cohort consists of 600 men, one-tenth of a legion. In Palestine the cohorts had 760 soldiers along with 240 mounted calvary. The cohorts usually protected border of frontier regions. In Jerusalem the cohort was stationed in the fortress of Antonia.

Corinth: The chief commercial city and capital of the Roman province of Achaia on the Isthmus of Corinth.

The famed temple of Aphrodite with its 1,000 temple prostitutes attests to its immorality. Here the Christian church flourished (Acts 18:1; 19:1; 1 Corinthians 1:2; 2 Corinthians 1:1, 23).

Cornelius: A centurion of the Holian Cohort stationed in Caesarea. He was a God-fearer, a Gentile who worshipped with Jews but was not yet a convert. He was respected by Jews and offered an excellent means by which the gospel could extend from Jews to Gentiles.

Crete: Large island in the Mediterranean Sea, southeast of Greece. From here Jews went to Jerusalem (Acts 2:11). Titus was appointed here to supervise and counteract the Judaisers (Titus 1:5-14).

Cyprus: Island in the Mediterranean Sea about forty-one miles south of Asia Minor (present-day Turkey). Famous for sources of copper. Paul and Barnabas encountered a magician there (Acts 13:4-12).

Damascus: A city in Syria in an oasis watered by rivers and canals. Mentioned several times in the Old Testament. It was a destination of Paul as there were many Christians there (Acts 9:2).

Demetrius: The leader and chief spokesman for silversmiths in Ephesus. When his livelihood was threatened by Paul's Christian preaching he incited the guild to riot.

Derbe: A town in central Asia Minor, in the district of Lycaonia. Paul visited here twice, establishing a Christian congregation during the first visit (Acts 14:6, 20). Gaius, one of Paul's disciples, came from Derbe (Acts 20:4).

Drusilla: Mentioned in Acts 23:24; third daughter of Agrippa I. Felix, procurator of Judea in A.D. 52–60, fell in love with her and wanted to marry her, and she left her husband for him.

Ephesus: Large seaport city in the Roman province of Asia, a commercial and religious center. Paul preached here for an extended period of time (Acts 19:8, 10). In the theater a riot broke out, instigated by Demetrius (Acts 19:23-41).

Epicureans: Followers of a Greek philosophy founded in the fourth century B.C. by Epicurus. In reaction to a stern religion, he believed that the chief goal of life is happiness, free from fear of death or of the gods. He did not believe in the life to come.

Felix: Antonius Felix, the Roman procurator of Judea in the years A.D. 52–60. He ruled during Paul's final visit to and arrest in Jerusalem.

Galatia: A region and Roman province of central Asia Minor (Acts 16:6; 18:23; 1 Corinthians 16:1; Galatians 1:2; 2 Timothy 4:10; 1 Peter 1:1).

Galilee: Northernmost area of Israel. Almost all of Jesus' ministry was in Galilee. Capernaum was a major city in this area.

Gamaliel: The grandson of Rabbi Hillel. He counseled moderation in response to Peter (Acts 5:34-39). He was a highly respected Pharisee in the Sanhedrin, and was also Paul's teacher (22:3).

Gentile: The term stems from the Hebrew word meaning nations (other than Israel). In the New Testament it describes peoples other than Jews. This vast population offered Christianity a rich mission field to which the Holy Spirit directed the church.

Glossalalia: The technical term to describe pneumatic or ecstatic utterances, or *speaking in tongues*. These are unintelligible unless interpreted. Frequently associated with the presence of the Holy Spirit.

God-fearer: A Gentile who worships with Jews but is not yet a convert.

Greek: The language of the New Testament. Common Greek was used by Paul in his writing. Also a term used to describe the European, or Gentile.

Hellenists: Greek-speaking Jews (Acts 6:1; 9:29), as opposed to Jews who spoke Hebrew or Aramaic. A term used to describe foreigners (Acts 2:5-6). Hellenists were in conflict with Jews who spoke Hebrew (Acts 6-7).

Herod Agrippa I: Grandson of Herod the Great. Persecuted the early church (Acts 12:1-23). He killed James and arrested Peter, who was released from jail by an angel.

Iconium: A city in south central Asia Minor. Visited by

Paul and Barnabas on the first journey, where Paul was threatened by both Jews and Gentiles (Acts 13-16; 2 Timothy 3:11).

James: One of the sons of Zebedee, and, with his brother John, one of the twelve disciples called by Jesus. He was one of the special group Jesus formed. Mentioned also as the son of Alphaeus.

Jerusalem: Chief city in Palestine, sacred to both Jews and Christians. The name implies foundation of shalom/peace. Became a major city due to David's political decisions.

Jew: Biblical term for persons who worshipped Yahweh after the Exile. In the New Testament it is used in contrast to Gentiles, Samaritans, and proselytes.

Joppa: The city to which Peter was summoned. Some thirty-five miles from Jerusalem, the city offers a small harbor on the Mediterranean Sea. It was destroyed during the Jewish uprising of A.D. 68.

Judea: Southern part of west Palestine. A small area around Jerusalem governed by Nehemiah after the Exile.

Judas: One of the twelve disciples. Betrayed Jesus for thirty pieces of silver. The motive for his betrayal has been argued by scholars and others for centuries. Traditions vary as to how he died.

Julius (of the Augustan Cohort): Assigned to guard Paul during the voyage to Rome. He treated Paul well, even allowing him to visit with friends at Sidon. He also protected Paul when other soldiers wanted to kill him.

Luke: Companion of Paul; physician; author of the third Gospel and Acts. Gentile by birth. His Gospel is marked by broad concerns: compassion for the poor, concern for women, cosmopolitan interests. He is symbolized by an ox, based on Ezekiel 1:10.

Lydda: City in the plain of Sharon about eleven miles south of Joppa. The site of one of the earliest apostolic miracles, the healing of the cripple (Acts 9:32).

Lystra: A town in central Asia Minor. Paul and Barnabas fled to this town (Acts 14:6-21). People were friendly until Jews from Antioch and Iconium created further disturbances.

Macedonia: Area north of Achaia, modern-day Balkan peninsula. Mountainous region containing the cities of Philippi and Thessalonica. A major land route between east and west.

Malta: An island in the Mediterranean Sea south of Cicily. It is about eighteen miles long and eight miles wide and offers excellent protection for sailing vessels. Paul landed there in mid-October during his voyage to Rome.

Matthias: An apostle chosen to replace Judas. He is believed to have suffered martyrdom.

Messiah: The God-appointed king at the end of time and eschatological hope. Literally it means *the anointed one*, from the Hebrew word meaning *to anoint*. The suffering messiah was unknown in late Judaism and therefore is the scandal of the New Testament.

Nazarene: A name that is used only with reference to Jesus. In Acts it refers to a sect within the Christian movement. When used by a Jew it has a derogatory connotation.

Nazirites: From the verb meaning to consecrate. These special people let their hair grow, and drank no strong drink or wine. They were sacred persons with a strong loyalty to God. Samson was a Nazirite, which accounted for his need to protect his hair.

Paphos: A city in southwestern Cyprus. Paul visited there during his first journey (Acts 13:6, 13).

Passover: The word means *to be spared*. It is the first of Judaism's great feasts, observed in the spring, commemorating the deliverance from Egypt. The term is used both for the feast and the ritual. Also called the feast of Unleavened Bread (Exodus 12:1–13:16; 23:15).

Pentecost: The fiftieth day after the Passover observation. For Christians it is the day when the gift of the Holy Spirit came (Acts 2:1). Therefore, Christians reinterpreted the meaning of the celebration in light of the Holy Spirit.

Perga: One of the leading cities in Pamphylia on the

southern coast of Asia Minor. Paul and Barnabas visited here during their first journey (Acts 13:13).

Pergamum: A city in Mysia, in western Asia Minor, where the church struggled against the emperor cult. Famous in Hellenistic times as a renowned center for art and learning (Revelation 1:11; 2:12).

Pharisee: A very important element in Judaism in New Testament times. Pharisees were legalists; they obeyed the letter of the Law. They did, however, believe in the doctrine of resurrection.

Philip: An apostle listed in Mark 3:18; Matthew 10:3; Luke 6:14; and Acts 1:13. One of the first disciples to be called, he brought Nathaniel to Jesus. He was mentioned in the feeding of the 5,000 (John 6:5-7) and was also an evangelist (Acts 21:8).

Philippi: A city in Macedonia. Paul founded a church here, the first Christian congregation established in Europe (Acts 16:11-40).

Phoenicia: A long (150 miles), narrow region north of Palestine along the east coast of the Mediterranean. Its people were seafaring merchants and shipbuilders.

Porcius Testus: The Roman procurator of Judea in the years A.D. 60–62; successor to Felix.

Proselyte: A term originally meaning a foreigner; a person not in his own land. In the New Testament the term is used to describe a convert to Judaism.

Ptolemais: A city in northern Palestine, north of Mt. Carmel. Modern-day Acre. Paul landed here during his third missionary journey (Acts 21:7).

Publius: Either the chief native official or high Roman authority on the island of Malta. Paul and his companions were hosted by Publius for three days. One tradition holds that he was later martyred.

Sabbath: From the Hebrew word meaning *cessation, desistance*. The closing day of a seven-day week. It means *rest*. In Jewish tradition it includes worship and prayer. Strict observance is required in the Old Testament decalogues (Ten Commandments). For Christians it became the first day of the week.

Sadducees: Priestly, aristocratic party in Judaism that emerged after the Maccabean Rebellion. They did not believe in the resurrection, Spirit, or angels, and became opponents of the Pharisees.

Salamis: A major city of Cyprus on the east coast opposite Syria. Paul and Barnabas visited the Jewish community there (Acts 13:5). According to tradition Barnabas was martyred there by a mob stirred up by Syrian Jews.

Samaria: The capital city of the Northern Kingdom, Israel. Also the region of the hill country of Palestine. After the deportations of 721 B.C. the Assyrians resettled the area with captives from Babylon, Cuthah, Avva, Hamath, and Sepharvaim (2 Kings 17:24-26).

Samaritans: Origins in Samaria, therefore decendants of the colonists (2 Kings 17). They were not full-fledged members of the house of Israel.

Sanhedrin: The seventy-one-member supreme Jewish council during the post-exilic period. It was an aristocratic unit until the fall of Jerusalem to the Romans in A.D. 70. This was the group responsible for internal government of the Roman-occupied territory of Palestine (Acts 23:1-10).

Simon, the magician: A man who had impressed Samaritans with his powers (Acts 8:9-24). When he saw the power of the Holy Spirit he wanted the power and offered to buy it. Because of this, the attempt to purchase church office is called simony. Even though a negative connotation is attached to his name, he did become a Christian and was baptized.

Stephen: The first Christian martyr at the hands of the Jews in Jerusalem (Acts 6:1–8:3). The details surrounding his death introduce the figure of Saul (Paul), who witnessed the stoning (Acts 7:58; 8:1).

Stoics: Followers of a philosophy prevalent throughout the Roman Empire. Founded in Athens by Zeno, this philosophy holds that virtue is good and vice is the only evil. Stoics steeled themselves against feeling pain or pleasure, success, or failure. Paul echoes part of this philosophy in Philippians 4:11-12.

Syria: Area bounded by the Mediterranean, Galilee, and the Arabian Desert. Had great influence on Palestine. Paul's conversion took place here, on the road to Damascus.

Tarsus: A city in Asia Minor, the capital of the province of Cilicia. Located on the Tarsus River, the city is about 6,000 years old. It had a large Jewish element. It was Paul's hometown.

Temple: A permanent building to replace the Tabernacle. First built by Solomon in Jerusalem (1 Kings 5–8; 2 Chronicles 2–7; Ezekiel 40–43). Later rebuilt by Zerubbabel, and finally by Herod, all on the present site of the Dome of the Rock, the Moslem place of worship in Jerusalem.

Theophilus: Person to whom Luke addressed the books of Luke and Acts (Luke 1:3; Acts 1:1). The name means *lover of God*. The identity of the person is not known.

Thessalonica: An important city in Macedonia. Paul established the church here after beatings in Philippi (Acts 16:22-24; 1 Thessalonians 2:2), and later wrote two letters to the congregation.

Thyatira: A city in western Asia Minor. One of Paul's associates may have gone there during a preaching mission in Ephesus (Acts 19:10). There was a strong church in Thyatira (Revelation 2:18-29).

Timothy: Trusted associate and friend of Paul; ranks with the apostles (1 Thessalonians 2:6). Sent by Paul to strengthen Gentile churches (Philippians 2:19), he first appeared as a disciple in Lystra (Acts 16:1).

Tyre: An important trade and port city on the Phoenician coast about twelve miles south of Sidon. In ancient times it was a very important producer of purple dye. Jesus preached here (see Mark 3:8; Luke 6:17). Paul stayed with the small Christian congregation for a week during his voyage to Rome.

Guide to Pronunciation

Achaia: Ah-KAY-ah
Adramyttium: Ah-drah-MIH-tee-um
Aeneas: Ah-NEE-us
Agabus: AH-gah-bus
Agrippa :Ah-GRIP-ah
Ananias: Ah-nah-NIGH-us
Antioch: AN-tee-ock
Areopagus: Air-ee-OP-ah-gus
Artemis: AHR-teh-miss
Caesarea: Sess-ah-REE-ah
Caiaphus: KAY-ah-fuss
Chaldeans: Kal-DEE-ans
Cilicia: Si-LEE-shuh
Cornelius: Kor-NEE-lee-us
Cyprus: SIGH-press
Cyrenians: Sigh-REE-nee-ans
Damascus: Dah-MASS-kus
Demetrius: Di-MEE-tree-us
Dorcus: DOR-kus
Ephesus: EH-feh-sus
Epicurean: Eh-pih-CURE-ee-an
Ethiopian: Ee-thee-OH-pee-an
Eunuch: YOO-nick
Eutychus: YOO-tih-kus
Galatia: Ga-LAY-shuh
Gamaliel: Ga-MAY-lee-el
Gentile: JEN-tile
Glossalalia: Gloss-a-LAY-lee-ah
Haran: Hah-RAHN

Hellenists: HEL-eh-nists
Hermes: HER-meez
Iconium: Eye-KO-nee-um
Joppa: JAH-pah
Judea: Joo-DEE-ah
Levite: LEE-vite
Lydda: LID-ah
Lystra: LIS-trah
Macedonia: Ma-seh-DO-nee-ah
Mount Sinai: Mount SIGH-nigh
Nazareth: NAZ-a-reth
Nicanor: NIGH-kan-or
Niger: NIGH-jer
Pamphylia: Pam-FILL-ee-ah
Paphos: PAF-ohs
Parmenas: PAR-men-as
Pentecost: PEN-te-kost
Perga: PER-gah
Phoenicia: Fo-NEE-shuh
Phrygia: FRIH-jee-ah
Pisidia: Pih-SIH-dee-ah
Prochorus: PRO-kor-us
Proselytes: PRAH-sell-ites
Ptolemias: Tol-eh-MAY-us
Rhegium: RAY-jee-um
Rhoda: RO-dah
Sadducees: SAD-ju-seez
Salmone: Sal-MOE-nay
Samaria: Sa-MARE-ee-ah
Sapphira: Sah-FEER-ah
Sergius Paulus: SER-jee-us-PAH-lus
Stoic: STOW-ick
Tabitha: TAB-ith-ah
Tarsus: TAR-sus
Tertullus: Ter-TULL-us
Theophilus: Thee-AH-fil-us
Thessalonica: Thess-a-loh-NIGH-kah
Timon: TIM-on
Trophimus: TROH-fih-mus

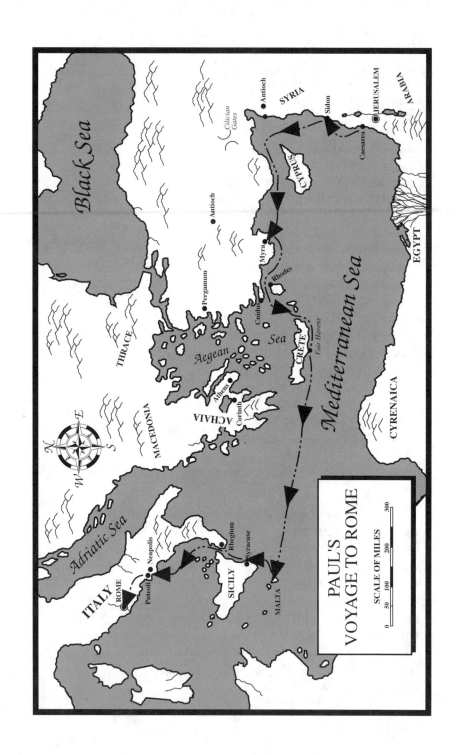

PAUL'S
VOYAGE TO ROME

SCALE OF MILES

0   50   100   200   300